starting out: the sicilian
the sicilian

JOHN EMMS

EVERYMAN CHESS

Gloucester Publishers plc   www.everymanchess.com

First published in 2002 by Gloucester Publishers plc, (formerly Everyman Publishers plc), Northburgh House, 10 Northburgh Street, London, EC1V 0AT

British Library Cataloguing-in-Publication Data
A catalogue record for this book is available from the British Library.

ISBN 1 85744 249 0

Distributed in North America by The Globe Pequot Press, P.O Box 480, 246 Goose Lane, Guilford, CT 06437-0480.

All other sales enquiries should be directed to Gloucester Publishers plc, Northburgh House, 10 Northburgh Street, London, EC1V 0AT
tel: 020 7253 7887 fax: 020 7490 3708
email: info@everymanchess.com
website: www.everymanchess.com

EVERYMAN CHESS SERIES (formerly Cadogan Chess)

Chief Advisor: Garry Kasparov
Commissioning Editor: Byron Jacobs

Typeset and edited by First Rank Publishing, Brighton.
Production by Navigator Guides.
Cover Design by Horatio Monteverde.
Printed and bound in Great Britain by The Cromwell Press Ltd

Everyman Chess

Starting Out Opening Guides:

1 85744 234 2	Starting Out: The King's Indian	Joe Gallagher
1 85744 229 6	Starting Out: The French	Byron Jacobs
1 85744 254 7	Starting Out: The Nimzo-Indian	Chris Ward

Books for players serious about improving their game:

1 85744 226 1	Starting Out in Chess	Byron Jacobs
1 85744 231 8	Tips for Young Players	Matthew Sadler
1 85744 236 9	Improve Your Opening Play	Chris Ward
1 85744 241 5	Improve Your Middlegame Play	Andrew Kinsman
1 85744 246 6	Improve Your Endgame Play	Glenn Flear
1 85744 223 7	Mastering the Opening	Byron Jacobs
1 85744 228 8	Mastering the Middlegame	Angus Dunnington
1 85744 233 4	Mastering the Endgame	Glenn Flear
1 85744 238 5	Simple Chess	John Emms
1 85744 115 X	Learn Chess: A Complete Course	Alexander & Beach
1 85744 072 2	How to Win at Chess	Daniel King
1 85744 297 0	Concise Chess Openings	Neil McDonald

Popular puzzle books:

1 85744 273 3	Multiple Choice Chess	Graeme Buckley
1 85744 296 2	It's Your Move	Chris Ward
1 85744 278 4	It's Your Move (Improvers)	Chris Ward

Contents

Bibliography

Books

Accelerated Dragons, John Donaldson & Jeremy Silman (Everyman 1998)

Beating the Sicilian 3, John Nunn & Joe Gallagher (Batsford 1995)

c3 Sicilian, Joe Gallagher (Everyman 1999)

Easy Guide to the Bb5 Sicilian, Steffen Pedersen (Everyman 1999)

Easy Guide to the Najdorf, Tony Kosten (Everyman 1999)

Easy Guide to the Sicilian Scheveningen, Steffen Pedersen (Everyman 1998)

Easy Guide to the Sveshnikov Sicilian, Jacob Aagaard (Everyman 2000)

Encyclopaedia of Chess Openings volumes A-E (Informator 2001)

Improve Your Opening Play, Chris Ward (Everyman 2000)

Mastering the Opening, Byron Jacobs (Everyman 2001)

Nunn's Chess Openings, John Nunn, Graham Burgess, John Emms & Joe Gallagher (Everyman/Gambit 1999)

Sicilian Grand Prix Attack, James Plaskett (Everyman 2000)

Sicilian Kalashnikov, Jan Pinski & Jacob Aagaard (Everyman 2001)

The Closed Sicilian, Daniel King (Chess Press 1997)

The Complete Najdorf: 6 Bg5, John Nunn (Batsford 1996)

The Complete Richter-Rauzer, Peter Wells (Batsford 1998)

The Oxford Companion to Chess, David Hooper and Kenneth Whyld (Oxford 1996)

The Taimanov Sicilian, Graham Burgess (Gambit 2000)

Winning with the Sicilian Dragon 2, Chris Ward (Batsford 2001)

Periodicals

ChessBase Magazine

Informator

The Week in Chess

Introduction

It's probably safe to say that the Sicilian Defence is the most famous chess opening of all time. It's certainly the most popular: almost a quarter of all games in chess are Sicilian Defences. This is a pretty large fraction considering the large pool of openings from which each player can choose. If you play 1 e4, the likelihood of facing a Sicilian Defence is approximately fifty percent.

Why the immense popularity? The easiest way to address this question is to take a look at some simple opening positions.

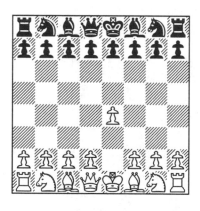

Diagram 1
White plays 1 e4

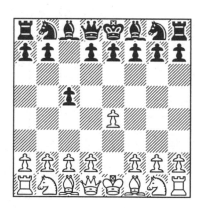

Diagram 2
Black plays the Sicilian

1 e4 is one of the two most popular opening moves for White (the other is 1 d4). With 1 e4 White gains some control over central squares and open lines of development for his queen and f1-bishop. Give White another free move and what would he like to play? The answer is 2 d4!, which controls more central squares and opens a line of development for the c1-bishop. With control of the centre and open lines for easy development, White is assured of a good position from the opening moves.

Black has many possible replies to 1 e4, but only two of these both gain a foothold in the centre and dissuade White from carrying out his 'threat'. These two choices are 1...e5 (symmetrical king's pawn) and 1...c5 (the Sicilian). It's no coincidence that these are the two most popular defences to 1 e4, but what is interesting is that the Sicilian occurs twice as often as 1...e5.

Let's take a look at the position after 1...c5 (Diagram 2).

Black has taken control of the crucial d4-square and is ready to answer d2-d4 with ...cxd4, thus eliminating one of White's central pawns and lessening White's control of the centre. The 'advantage' the Sicilian has over, say, 1...e5 is that Black is able to unbalance the position with an asymmetrical pawn structure from a very early stage. This allows both sides the opportunity to play for a win from the very start. White is less likely to acquire a 'risk free' edge because the position will always contain some imbalance.

Pawn Structures

Two-thirds of this book deals with 'Open Sicilian' positions, in which White plays 2 Nf3 followed by 3 d4. This is by far the most common way for White to meet the Sicilian. White opens more lines of development and attempts to exploit the fact that he will be ahead on development.

Let's take a look at the possible opening moves 1 e4 c5 2 Nf3 d6 3 d4 cxd4 4 Nxd4 (Diagram 3)

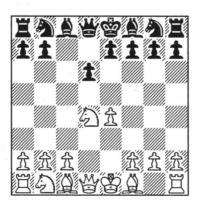

Diagram 3
An Open Sicilian

White is ahead in development and can develop more freely. Black, however, has a structural advantage in that he has an extra central pawn, which gives him long-term chances of taking control of the centre. A typical imbalance has arisen. The onus is on White to use his development advantage in order to secure an early initiative. If White plays passively or his initiative runs out of steam, then typically it's Black, with the better pawn structure, who has the long-term chances. Thus it's quite rare for a state of 'dull equality' to arise. Often in a Sicilian, if Black 'equalises', he is already slightly better! This structural advantage is seen in most Open Sicilian lines: for example, the Dragon, the Najdorf and the Scheveningen Variations. The major exception to this rule is the Sveshnikov Variation, in which Black accepts pawn weaknesses for activity.

Variations

A word on how this book is set out. In the first five chapters we shall be taking a look at the most common variations of the Open Sicilian: the Dragon, the Najdorf, the Scheveningen, the Sveshnikov and the Classical. There are naturally many similar characteristics to these variations but they all contain their own distinctive flavour. In Chapter 6 we move on to slightly less common variations of the Open Sicilian: the Taimanov, the Accelerated Dragon, the Four Knights, the Kan and the Kalashnikov. In Chapters 7-9 we study lines where White avoids the complexities of the Open Sicilian in favour of quieter lines. These include Bb5 systems (Chapter 7), early c2-c3 systems (Chapter 8) and finally some more unusual systems white systems (Chapter 9).

Just to give you an insight into how much 'theory' has amassed on the Sicilian over the years, I'm currently holding a heavyweight 320-page monograph written not on the Sicilian, or even a variation of the Sicilian, but on a sub-variation of a variation of the Sicilian! By covering all the main lines of the Sicilian, it wasn't my intention to give a vast collection of theory, nor to arm the reader with a white or black repertoire. This book very much aims to be an introduction to the main lines and ideas of the Sicilian and to help readers choose variations they think will suit their style. I've used illustrative games that show some of the more entertaining and instructive Sicilian battles, not necessarily ones which reflect the current state of theory.

Finally, I would like to thank Byron Jacobs for his help on this project and special thanks go to Christine for her proof-reading, patience and support as the deadline approached.

John Emms,
Kent,
April 2002

The Dragon Variation

1 e4 c5 2 Nf3 d6 3 d4 cxd4 4 Nxd4 Nf6 5 Nc3 g6 (Diagram 1)

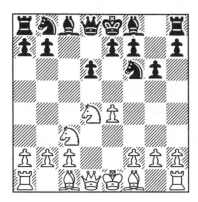

Diagram 1
The starting position for the Sicilian Dragon

The Dragon Variation is the Sicilian in its most natural and logical form. Black develops his pieces on their most active squares. In particular, the 'Dragon bishop' is fianchettoed on the long diagonal, down which it exerts its significant presence.

It's possible that the Dragon derived its name from the shape made by Black's pawn island from the d- to h-files. Its name is certainly consistent with the type of chess it produces: aggressive, cut-throat and fearsome. This line of the Sicilian is not for the faint-hearted!

The Dragon has been around for over a century. It was first used in the 1880s by the renowned openings theoretician Louis Paulsen and it was also taken up by Harry Nelson Pillsbury, one of the world's leading players at the turn of the century. Nowadays it has supporters at every level of chess and in 1995 it received an ultimate seal of approval when Garry Kasparov utilised it with great success in his world championship match with Vishy Anand.

The Yugoslav Attack

1 e4 c5 2 Nf3 d6 3 d4 cxd4 4 Nxd4 Nf6 5 Nc3 g6 6 Be3

This bishop move, further developing the queenside, signifies that White intends to play the Yugoslav Attack. This line (which is sometimes also referred to as the 'Rauzer Attack') occurred a few times in the 1930s in the Soviet Union and was later refined by leading Yugoslav players.

I can safely say that the Yugoslav Attack is the ultimate test of the Dragon. White quickly develops his queenside and castles long before turning his attentions to an all-out assault on the black king. To the untrained eye, this attack can look both awesome and unnerving.

6...Bg7

Attacking the bishop with 6...Ng4?? is a bad mistake as the reply 7 Bb5+! wins material after either 7...Nc6 8 Nxc6 bxc6 9 Bxc6+ Bd7 10 Bxa8 or 7...Bd7 8 Qxg4 (the bishop on d7 is pinned).

7 f3

Preventing the annoying possibility of ...Ng4 and thus preparing Qd2 and 0-0-0.

7...0-0 8 Qd2 Nc6 9 Bc4

Another major possibility for White is the immediate 9 0-0-0, not expending time with the manoeuvre Bc4-b3. This can give White extra time to conduct his attack. However, this also gives Black the extra option of an immediate strike in the centre with 9...d5!? (see Game 3).

9...Bd7 10 0-0-0 (Diagram 2)

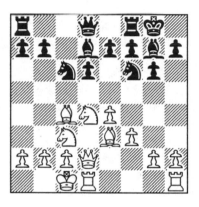

Diagram 2
A normal starting position in the Yugoslav Attack

Strategies

White plans the following:

1) Prise open the h-file with h2-h4-h5, perhaps supported by g2-g4.

2) Exchange off Black's main defenders on the kingside. The Dragon bishop on g7 can be exchanged with Be3-h6. The defensive knight on f6 can be exchange or eliminated in a number of ways, including Nd5 and g4-g5.

Put another way, in the words of Bobby Fischer, 'pry open the h-file, sac, sac ... mate!'

Black plans to gain counterplay on the queenside with moves such as ...Ra8-c8, ...Ne5-c4, ...b7-b5 and ...Qd8-a5. Sometimes Black sacrifices a rook for knight with ...Rc8xc3, disrupting the pawn structure around the white king. Defensively, Black can consider halting the advance of White's h-pawn with ...h7-h5. Although this allows White to continue an attack with g2-g4, this is sometimes more difficult to arrange. If given time, Black may move the f8-rook, a point of which is to answer Bh6 with ...Bh8. This allows Black to keep the 'Dragon bishop', which does such a good job along the long diagonal both in defence and attack.

Compared to the other variations in the Dragon, the Yugoslav Attack is by far the most tactical and dynamic. Mating combinations and sacrifices are the order of the day as both players go for an early kill. Positional play rarely enters the fray but is more likely if the queens are exchanged early. This can sometimes be achieved if an early ...Qd8-a5 is answered by Nc3-d5, offering an exchange on d2.

Theoretical?

The Yugoslav Attack is perhaps the most theoretically complex line of all openings. General principles are useful, but in this opening there is no substitute for learning the seemingly endless amount of critical variations. If you wish to play the Dragon then you need to be thoroughly prepared for all of White's options in the Yugoslav Attack. This means a lot of hard work, but the reward for the well-prepared can be many easily obtained points.

Statistics

Because of the excitement it brings, the Yugoslav Attack is fantastically popular at all levels of chess. The diagram position above has been reached literally thousands of times in international chess. According to *Mega Database 2002* (a database of over two million top class games), White scores around 55%, just one per cent above average. The most revealing statistic is that over 75% of all games in the Yugoslav are decisive (the normal figure is around 65%).

Illustrative Games

Game 1
□ **Minic** ■ **P.Lee**
Krakow 1964

1 e4 c5 2 Nf3 d6 3 d4 cxd4 4 Nxd4 Nf6 5 Nc3 g6 6 Be3 Bg7 7 f3 0-0 8 Qd2 Nc6 9 Bc4 Bd7 10 0-0-0 Rc8

Beginning counterplay on the half-open c-file.

10...Qa5 is another popular line, championed by the English grandmaster and Dragon expert Chris Ward. In this variation Black plans to shift his f8-rook to c8, thus allowing the option of meeting Bh6 with ...Bh8.

11 Bb3

Sensible play. The bishop moves out of the line of fire on the c-file.

11...Ne5

Unleashing the rook and preparing ...Ne5-c4.

12 h4

Here comes that h-pawn! Now Black has two major alternatives.

12...Nc4

Another major possibility for Black here is 12...h5 (see Game 2).

13 Bxc4

It is generally better for White to give up the light-squared bishop for this knight; the other bishop is needed to exchange off black's 'Dragon bishop'.

13...Rxc4 14 h5

The slower 14 g4, preparing h4-h5 without sacrifice, is also possible.

Exercise 1: What's wrong with the immediate 14 Bh6, offering a trade of dark-squared bishops?

14...Nxh5 15 g4

The point: White has sacrificed a pawn to open the h-file and gain time for the attack by hassling the knight.

15...Nf6 16 Bh6!? (Diagram 3)

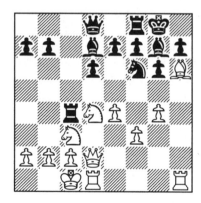

Diagram 3
White offers a trade

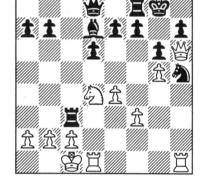

Diagram 4
How does White continue?

This move leads to great complications.

16...Bxh6?

It's a sure sign of a razor sharp system when a natural-looking move simply loses out of hand.

WARNING: One slip by either side in the Yugoslav Attack is often decisive.

The move 16...Nxe4!, unleashing the 'Dragon bishop' in an attack on d4, is the theoretical recommendation. Of course, there are an incredible number of tries for both sides but decades of experience has shown that the critical line is 17 Qe3! Rxc3 (shattering the pawns on the queenside) 18 bxc3 Nf6 19 Bxg7 Kxg7 with a very unclear position. White is the exchange for a pawn ahead and still has chances to attack down the h-file. White's own king, however, is looking very airy and Black can unleash a quick counter with ...Qa5 and ...Rc8. Notice that 20 Qh6+ Kh8! 21 g5 Nh5 defends for Black, for example: 22 Rxh5 gxh5 23 Rh1 Rg8 24 Rxh5 Rg7 and White's attack has reached a dead end.

17 Qxh6 Rxc3

A logical response. Black gives up his rook for a knight in order to prevent Nd5 and ruin the pawn structure around the white king. This is such a typical shot for Black in the Dragon. Here, unfortunately, it arrives too late.

18 g5!

White simply ignores the rook; the attack down the h-file will be devastating.

18...Nh5 (Diagram 4) 19 Rxh5!

Eliminating Black's final defender.

19...gxh5 20 Rh1

Despite being a rook ahead, Black has no defence to the mating attack along the h-file.

20...Qc8

Or 20...f6 21 g6! hxg6 22 Qxg6+ Kh8 23 Rxh5 mate.

21 Rxh5 Bf5 22 exf5 Rxc2+ 23 Nxc2 Qxf5 24 g6! Black resigns

A final tactic. 24...Qxg6 25 Rg5 wins the queen and leaves Black hopelessly behind on material.

Game 2
☐ **Koval** ■ **Berman**
Correspondence 1985

1 e4 c5 2 Nf3 d6 3 d4 cxd4 4 Nxd4 Nf6 5 Nc3 g6 6 Be3 Bg7 7 f3 Nc6 8 Qd2 0-0 9 Bc4 Bd7 10 h4 Rc8 11 Bb3 h5 12 0-0-0 Ne5

Via a slightly different move-order, we've reached the main position where Black plays ...h7-h5, preventing White from playing h4-h5.

13 Bg5

Moving the bishop to an active square and preparing kingside operations. Of course, White has many ways to conduct the attack: he can also continue with the ultra-aggressive 13 g4 or 13 Bh6, or play a preparatory defensive move such as 13 Kb1.

13...Rc5

As well as pressure down the c-file, the rook can also be used for defensive purposes on the fourth rank.

14 g4!?

White goes 'all in'.

14...hxg4 15 Bxf6?

A fundamental mistake. White eliminates a black defender but now there will be no way of getting rid of Black's powerful 'Dragon bishop'.

WARNING: Be very wary of exchanging the dark-squared bishop for a knight in the Dragon. Unless this leads to something concrete, this is rarely a good idea (this applies to both White and Black).

Further sacrificing with 15 h5, leading to massive complications, is the way forward.

15...Bxf6 16 h5 g5!

Refusing to open the h-file.

17 Nd5 Rxd5!

Another example of an effective exchange sacrifice. White's powerful knight is eliminated from the board.

18 exd5 gxf3 19 c3 g4

White's attack has reached a dead end on the kingside. Slowly but surely, Black takes over the operation.

20 Kb1 Qb6 21 Bc2 Nc4 22 Qc1 Rc8 23 Nf5? (Diagram 5)

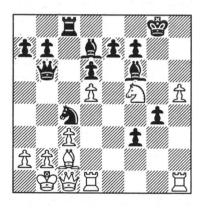

Diagram 5
Black has a winning tactic

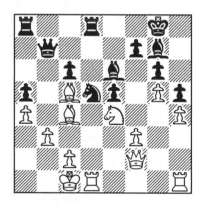

Diagram 6
White has a strong bishop on c5

Allowing a deadly combination.

23...Na3+ 24 Ka1 Rxc3! 25 Nxe7+ Kf8 White resigns

Black mates after 26 bxc3 Bxc3+, while White's position collapses after 26 Rh2 f2.

Game 3
□ **Almasi** ■ **Watson**
German Bundesliga 1995

---

1 e4 c5 2 Nf3 d6 3 d4 cxd4 4 Nxd4 Nf6 5 Nc3 g6 6 Be3 Bg7 7 f3

0-0 8 Qd2 Nc6 9 0-0-0

White hopes to gain time to use in the kingside attack by delaying (or leaving out) the development of the bishop to c4. If Black simply develops as normal this extra time can be very advantageous to White.

9...d5!?

This is what White's last move allows. Now there are some exchanges in the centre.

10 exd5 Nxd5 11 Nxc6 bxc6 12 Bd4

The positional approach, offering the trade of dark-squared bishops.

White can win a pawn here with 12 Nxd5 cxd5 13 Qxd5, but after 13...Qc7 the open files on the queenside give Black plenty of attacking chances. Note that 14 Qxa8 Bf5! wins the queen. After 15 Qxf8+ Kxf8 Black still has a strong attack.

12...e5 13 Bc5 Be6!

Another typical offer of an exchange sacrifice in the Dragon.

14 Ne4!

After 14 Bxf8 Qxf8 most experts agree that Black's attacking chances and dark square control more than make up for the slight material deficit. Note that Black already threatens ...Bh6, pinning the white queen to the king. Indeed, Dragon expert and Grandmaster Eduard Gufeld has won at least once in this fashion!

NOTE: Exchange sacrifices are very common in the Yugoslav Attack.

14...Re8 15 g4 h6 16 h4 a5 17 g5 h5 18 a4 Qc7 19 Bc4 Red8 20 Qf2 Qb7 21 b3 (Diagram 6)

Play is slower here than in the other games in the Yugoslav, as both the kingside and the queenside are partially blocked.

21...Nf4 22 Bxe6 Nxe6 23 Rxd8+! Rxd8 24 Bb6 Ra8 25 Rd1 Nd4 26 Bc5 Qd7 27 Nf6+ Bxf6 28 gxf6 Qf5?

A mistake. Correct is 28...Rd8!, after which 29 Rd3?? Nxb3+! 30 Rxb3 Qd1+ 31 Kb2 Rd2 (Almasi) gives Black a winning attack.

29 Bxd4 exd4 30 Qxd4 Qxf3 31 Qe5!

Now White is breaking through on the kingside.

31...Qf2 32 Rd7! Rf8 33 Kb2 c5 34 Rxf7! Black resigns

A nice combination to finish the game. White mates after both 34...Kxf7 35 Qe7+ Kg8 36 Qg7 and 34...Rxf7 35 Qe8+ Rf8 36 Qxg6+ Kh8 37 Qg7.

The Classical Variation

1 e4 c5 2 Nf3 d6 3 d4 cxd4 4 Nxd4 Nf6 5 Nc3 g6 6 Be2

While it's true that the Yugoslav Attack is the crucial test of the Dragon, playing in such a flamboyant way does not suit everyone's tastes. For the more peacefully inclined, the Classical Variation is an ideal choice. White simply develops in a 'classical' manner and castles kingside.

6...Bg7 7 0-0 Nc6 (Diagram 7)

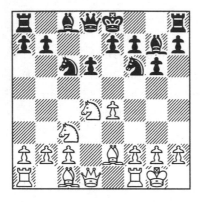

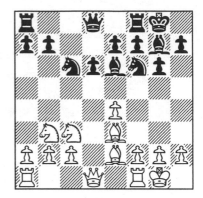

Diagram 7	**Diagram 8**
A starting position for the Classical	A typical Classical position

Adding early pressure onto d4. Now White must be wary of tactics.

8 Be3

This is logical, supporting the knight on d4, but let's also look at a couple of alternatives:

a) 8 f4? (White neglects to deal with the threat) 8...Nxe4! (unleashing the power of the bishop) 9 Nxc6 (9 Nxe4 Nxd4 also wins a pawn) 9...Qb6+ 10 Kh1 Nxc3 11 bxc3 bxc6 and Black has won a vital pawn.

NOTE: In the Dragon Black has many tactics available to exploit the pressure along the long a1-h8 diagonal.

b) 8 Nb3 chooses at once to move the knight away from the crossfire in the centre. After 8...0-0 White often continues with 9 Bg5, a line which was made popular by Karpov in the late 1970s (see Game 4).

8...0-0 9 Nb3

Again removing the knight from the centre, thus eliminating annoying tactics for Black. A semi-waiting move such as 9 Kh1 is met directly by the strategically desirable advance 9...d5!. Following 10 exd5 Nxd5 11 Nxd5 Qxd5 12 Bf3 Qa5 13 Nxc6 bxc6 14 Bxc6 Rb8 Black is extremely active.

Beginning a kingside offensive with 9 f4!? looks logical, but Black can exploit the weaknesses in White's position with the dangerous 9...Qb6 The theory is rather complex but Black is more than holding his own.

NOTE: White should normally try to prevent the ...d6-d5 advance.

9...Be6 (Diagram 8)

A good square for the bishop, pointing menacingly at the queenside.

Strategies

The stage is set for an interesting positional battle. White tries to keep a firm grip on the central squares (especially d5) and can play aggressively with f2-f4-f5 and even g2-g4-g5. These lunges, however, are double-edged. If White is not careful then he can leave himself overextended and vulnerable to counter-attack.

Black's best chance of counterplay lies in the half-open c-file and the possibility of pushing the a- and b-pawns. He may seek to place a piece on the desirable c4-square and this can be achieved, for example, with ...Rc8, ...Ne5 (a5) and ...Nc4 (or Bc4). At any time Black will be looking to see if he can carry out a favourable ...d6-d5 advance.

The Classical Variation gives rise to very much more strategic play than the Yugoslav Attack. White still concentrates mainly on the kingside (and Black on the other wing), but the respective attacks are more restrained and are more of a space-gaining exercise rather than an all-out mating attack. The Classical appeals to more positionally minded white players.

Theoretical?

The Classical Variation is much less theoretical than the Yugoslav Attack and players are more likely to be able to get away with just playing on general principles.

Statistics

Everything else dwarfs in comparison to the popularity of the Yugoslav Attack, but it's safe to say that the Classical Variation comes a safe second. According to *Mega Database 2002*, Diagram 7 has been reached in over 1,200 games. Overall White scores around 52%, while 66% of the games are decisive.

Illustrative Games

Game 4
□ **Apicella** ■ **Svidler**
Yerevan Olympiad 1996

1 e4 c5 2 Nf3 d6 3 d4 cxd4 4 Nxd4 Nf6 5 Nc3 g6 6 Be2 Bg7 7 0-0 Nc6 8 Nb3 0-0 9 Bg5 a6

Black begins queenside operations.

10 f4 b5 11 Bf3

Threatening e4-e5, but Black has a natural response.

11...Bb7 12 Kh1

This is a common move in many Sicilian positions. The king is safer on h1 and White does not have to consistently calculate lines involving a queen check on b6.

12...Nd7 13 Rb1

Defending the b-pawn so that the knight on c3 can move to d5.

13...Re8 14 Nd5

Now White has annoying pressure against the e7-pawn. Black deals with this in a surprising way.

14...f6!

This move was discovered by the Brain Games World Champion, Vladimir Kramnik. It seems strange to block the Dragon bishop like this, but it seems that there are other positional factors which favour Black.

15 Bh4 e6 16 Ne3 g5! 17 Bg3

After 17 fxg5 fxg5 18 Bg3 Nde5 the 'Dragon bishop' has come to life and Black has acquired the e5-square as an important outpost.

NOTE: An outpost is a square which cannot easily be attacked by enemy pawns. The e5-square is often a useful outpost for Black in the Sicilian.

17...gxf4 18 Bxf4 Nde5 19 Bh5 Rf8 (Diagram 9)

Black's 'Dragon bishop' is hemmed in by the pawn on f6, but Black is extremely solid and has a good defensive outpost on e5.

20 c3 Qe7 21 Qe2 Ng6 22 Bg3 Nce5 23 Nd2 Kh8 24 Rf2 Rad8 25 Rbf1 Bh6

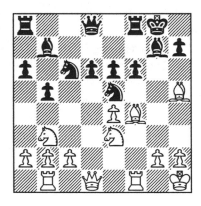
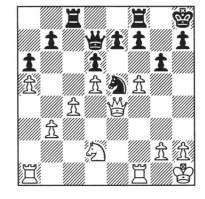

Diagram 9
Black is extremely solid

Diagram 10
White dictates matters

Now the dark-squared bishop is as active as its partner on b7.

26 Ng4?! Nxg4 27 Bxg4 d5!

Breaking up the centre and increasing the activity of his piece. Black is now firmly in control.

28 Bh5 dxe4 29 Nxe4 f5 30 Bxg6 hxg6 31 Nd6 Ba8!

31...Rxd6? loses material to 32 Qe5+!.

32 Be5+ Kg8 33 Rd1 Rd7 34 Qd3 Rfd8

The knight on d6 superficially looks impressive, but in fact it's quite vulnerable as it has no safe square to go to.

35 Qg3 Qg5 36 Qxg5 Bxg5 37 Rd3 Be4 38 Rh3 Rxd6 39 Rh8+ Kf7 40 Rh7+ Ke8 41 Rh8+ Kd7 White resigns

Following 42 Rxd8+ Bxd8 43 Bxd6 Kxd6 44 Rd2+ Ke7 the two bishops heavily outclass the rook in this endgame.

Game 5
☐ **Thipsay** ■ **Duncan**
London 1994

---

1 e4 c5 2 Nf3 d6 3 d4 cxd4 4 Nxd4 Nf6 5 Nc3 g6 6 Be2 Bg7 7 0-0 Nc6 8 Be3 0-0 9 Nb3 Be6 10 f4 Rc8 11 Kh1

White can play more aggressively with 11 f5, but after 11...Bd7 he must be careful not to overextend. After 11 f5 Bd7 12 g4?! Ne5! 13 g5 Rxc3! 14 bxc3 Nxe4 Black's pieces dominate the board.

NOTE: The ...Rxc3 exchange sacrifice is particularly effective if Black can also grab White's important central pawn.

11...Na5

Planning to make use of the c4-square. Black can also keep his options open with 11...a6, with the idea of ...b7-b5-b4.

12 f5 Nc4

Perhaps 12...Bc4 is stronger.

13 Bd4 Bd7 14 Bxc4 Rxc4 15 Qd3 Rc8 16 a4

White's extra space promises a small advantage.

16...a6 17 a5 Bc6 18 Nd2 Qd7?!

18...Qc7 prevents White's next move.

19 Nd5! Bxd5 20 exd5 Ng4 21 Bxg7 Kxg7 22 c4 Ne5 23 Qe4 Kh8 24 b3 (Diagram 10)

The pawn structure has changed in White's favour. Black no longer has counterplay on the queenside and White is free to concentrate on kingside operations.

24...Rg8 25 h3 Rg7 26 f6! exf6 27 Rxf6 Rgg8 28 Qd4 Rge8 29 Ne4 Qe7 30 Raf1 Rcd8 31 Rxf7 Qh4 32 Nf6 Qh6 33 Nxe8 Rxe8 34 R7f6 Black Resigns

The Levenfish Attack

1 e4 c5 2 Nf3 d6 3 d4 cxd4 4 Nxd4 Nf6 5 Nc3 g6 6 f4 (Diagram 11)

The Russian Grandmaster Grigory Levenfish developed this trappy line in the 1930s as an alternative to the tried and trusted Classical.

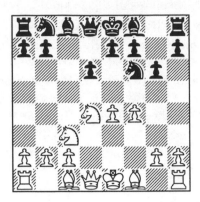

Diagram 11
The starting position for the Levenfish Attack

6...Nc6

6...Bg7!? is the most natural move in the position, but this allows White to complicate matters with 7 e5 (see Game 6).

7 Nxc6 bxc6 8 e5 Nd7 9 exd6 exd6

This leads us to Game 7.

Strategies

White hopes to catch Black cold with an early advance in the centre. Aided by the f-pawn, White quickly pushes his e-pawn to e5, dislodging Black's f6-knight and impeding Black's comfortable development.

Black's strategy must be to get through the opening few moves without any disasters occurring, which is sometimes easier said than done! However, if Black can negotiate these difficult early moves then he has a good chance of reaching a very promising position in the early middlegame.

The Levenfish often begins with a flurry of tactics. However, assuming Black gets through these without any harm, then the positions can become either tactical or strategic in nature.

Theoretical?

Black players are advised to methodically learn an acceptable defence to the Levenfish Attack. Refraining from this can lead to an early disaster and on this occasion one would rather not learn from an unpleasant experience!

Statistics

The Levenfish is not popular at the highest levels and there have been very few grandmaster games in the past few years. At lower levels, however, the Levenfish is both more popular and more successful; many inexperienced black players keep falling into one or other of the many pitfalls.

Illustrative Games

Game 6
□ **Pilnik** ■ **Kashdan**
New York 1948

1 e4 c5 2 Nf3 d6 3 d4 cxd4 4 Nxd4 Nf6 5 Nc3 g6 6 f4 Bg7 7 e5!

After this move Black must tread very carefully.

7...dxe5

Another option for Black is 7...Nh5. Now the move 8 g4? seems to trap the black knight. However, Black has the resource 8...Nxf4! 9 Bxf4 dxe5, regaining the piece with advantage. Instead of 8 g4, White should play 8 Bb5+ Bd7 9 e6!.

8 fxe5 Ng4?

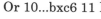

WARNING: The knight on g4 can be vulnerable to tactical shots in the opening.

8...Nfd7 9 c6 Nc5 is the best way for Black to continue. After 8...Ng4? White wins material by force.

9 Bb5+! (Diagram 12)

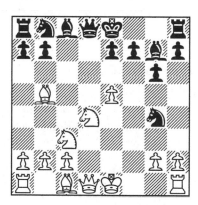

Diagram 12
Black is in trouble

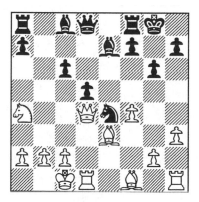

Diagram 13
Black's knight is a beast!

9...Nc6

The only move. Both 9...Bd7 and 9...Nd7 lose a piece to 10 Qxg4, while 9...Kf8? suffers a worse fate after 10 Ne6+! and 11 Qxd8.

10 Nxc6 Qxd1+

Or 10...bxc6 11 Bxc6+, followed by Bxa8.

11 Nxd1 a6 12 Ba4 Bd7 13 h3 Nh6

By pinning the knight to the bishop, Black regains his piece, but a little trick ensures that White remains a valuable pawn up.

14 Nxe7! Bxa4 15 Nd5 Rd8 16 c4 Nf5 17 Bg5 Rd7 18 N1c3 Bc6 19 0-0-0 h5

19...Bxe5 loses material to 20 Rhe1, setting up a deadly pin.

20 Nc7+! Kf8

20...Rxc7 allows mate in one with 21 Rd8.

21 Rxd7 Bxd7 22 Rd1

Black is forced to give up a piece. 22...Be8 loses to 23 Rd8.

22...Bxe5 23 Rxd7 h4 24 Ne4 Nd4 25 Rd8+ Kg7 26 Ne8+ Kh7 27 N4f6+ Bxf6 28 Nxf6+ Black resigns

---

Game 7
□ Illijin ■ Cebalo
Baden 1999

---

1 e4 c5 2 Nf3 d6 3 d4 cxd4 4 Nxd4 Nf6 5 Nc3 g6 6 f4 Nc6!

To a certain extent, this move avoids the tricks.

7 Nxc6

Or 7 Bb5 Bd7 8 Bxc6 bxc6 9 e5 Nd5 10 Nxd5 cxd5 11 exd6 e6! (Ward) and Black follows up with ...Bxd6.

White can play in a quiet manner with 7 Nf3!?, but this poses no real threat to the black position. Play is level after 7...Bg7 8 Bd3 0-0 9 0-0 Bg4.

7...bxc6 8 e5

White insists on the central breakthrough.

8...Nd7 9 exd6 exd6 10 Qd4

By attacking the rook in the corner and preparing to castle queenside, White keeps up the pace. Objectively, 10 Be2 is safer but hardly troublesome for Black.

10...Nf6 11 Be3 Be7!

An unusual occurrence in the Dragon; the bishop is developed on e7 rather than g7! However, there is a good reason; after 11...Bg7 12 0-0-0 d5 13 Qc5! Black has problems castling.

12 0-0-0 0-0 13 h3

Preventing ...Ng4.

13...d5 14 Na4?!

Preparing Nc5, but Black gets in first!

14...Ne4! (Diagram 13)

This is a powerful outpost for the black knight.

15 Be2 Be6

Black now has a very automatic attack on the queenside, with moves such as ...Qa5, ...Rb8 and ...Bf6 springing to mind. White's next move, sacrificing a pawn to clear lines, smacks of desperation.

16 f5 Bxf5 17 Bh6 Bf6! 18 Qe3 Re8 19 Qf4 Qa5 20 b3 Nc3 21 Bd3 Nxa2+ 22 Kb1 Nc3+ 23 Kc1 Re4 24 Qd6 Be7 25 Qxc6 Rc8 26 Qa6 Rxa4 27 bxa4 Ne2+ White resigns

It's mate after 28 Bxe2 Rxc2+ 29 Kb1 Qb4+ 30 Ka1 Qb2.

White Plays g2-g3

1 e4 c5 2 Nf3 d6 3 d4 cxd4 4 Nxd4 Nf6 5 Nc3 g6 6 g3 (Diagram 14)

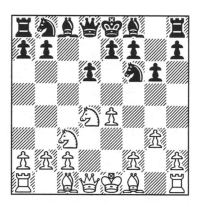

Diagram 14
The starting position for the g3 variation

This introduces a positional and sophisticated system of development which is, however, considered by most to be quite harmless against the Dragon. White expends an extra tempo to develop his kingside bishop on g2, where it will be blocked by the e4-pawn. When put like this, it is surprising that this line has gained any popularity at all. However, as we shall see below, there are some redeeming features to this method of development.

6...Nc6 7 Nde2

For 7 Bg2 Nxd4 8 Qxd4 Bg7 9 0-0 0-0, see Game 8.

7...Bg7 8 Bg2 0-0 9 0-0

Strategies

For once in the Dragon, White's play is not motivated by an attack on the black king. Instead, White normally aims for positional pressure on the centre.

The bishop on g2 overprotects the e4-pawn. This allows White's knight on c3 to move and a common idea for White is to play Nc3-d5, which can prove to be of great annoyance value. If Black captures on d5, then White normally recaptures with the e4-pawn, offering him the chance to utilise the newly formed half-open e-file. If instead Black attacks the knight with ...e7-e6, then this leaves the d6-pawn slightly vulnerable.

Again Black looks to the queenside for counterplay, although he must be careful not to advance his queenside pawns too early as this may allow White to unleash his light-squared bishop with e4-e5. Rather than acquiescing to an exchange, when the white knight reaches d5, Black generally tries to play around it before ejecting it with a timely ...e7-e6 (see Game 9).

Theoretical?

The g3 line of the Dragon is hardly theoretical and is often played by players who are looking to avoid a heavyweight theoretical battle. There are only one or two variations which need to be learnt.

Statistics

I would have said that this is not a particularly popular line, but I did find just over a thousand examples of Diagram 14 in *Mega Database 2002*, with White scoring a surprisingly high 60%. So perhaps g3 is an underestimated move against the Dragon!

At lower levels, however, I would imagine that this line is less popular as most players are lured by the rewards and the complications of the Yugoslav and Levenfish Attacks.

Illustrative Games

Game 8
□ **Adams** ■ **Kramnik**
Wijk aan Zee 1998

1 e4 c5 2 Nf3 Nc6 3 Nc3

White employs an unusual move order, but eventually we reach an Open Sicilian.

3...d6 4 d4 cxd4 5 Nxd4 Nf6 6 g3 g6

What started off as a Classical Sicilian, has now transposed into a Dragon.

NOTE: There are many transpositional possibilities in the Sicilian Defence.

7 Bg2 Nxd4

It's quite unusual for Black to exchange knights so early, but here Black believes that the queen may become vulnerable on d4.

8 Qxd4 Bg7 9 0-0 0-0 10 Qb4?!

Prophylactic thinking. White removes the queen from d4 before Black has a chance to take advantage of it. However, it turns out that the queen is just as vulnerable on this square. White should consider either 10 h3 Be6 11 Qd1 or 10 Qd3!?.

NOTE: Prophylaxis is the strategic idea of anticipating or preventing an opponent's threat before it exists.

10...a5! 11 Qb3 Be6! (Diagram 15)

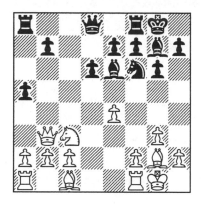 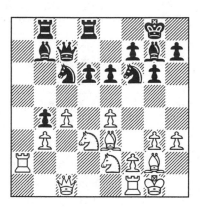

Diagram 15	**Diagram 16**
Inviting the queen to grab a hot pawn	Black misses a chance to complicate

Black offers a pawn sacrifice, tempting the queen deep into enemy territory.

12 Nd5

After 12 Qxb7 Nd7, in return for the pawn, Black is very active and White's queen is vulnerable.

12...a4!

Forcing the issue.

13 Qxb7 Nxd5 14 exd5 Bf5

White is a pawn up, but it's Black who stands better. Both the c2- and b2-pawns are vulnerable and White's queen is not well placed on b7.

15 Bg5 Qb8!

Even the endgame will favour Black.

16 Qxb8 Rfxb8 17 Bxe7 Rxb2 18 a3

Or 18 Bxd6 Rxc2 19 Rad1 Rxa2 (Kramnik) and Black's passed pawn is stronger than White's.

18...Rxc2 19 Rae1 Ra6

Protecting the vital d6-pawn. Now the major weakness in the position is White's a3-pawn.

20 Be4 Bxe4 21 Rxe4 Bb2 22 Rfe1?

22 Re3! limits the damage.

22...Rc1!

Now the a-pawn is lost. Note that 22...Bxa3?? allows 23 Bf6! with an unstoppable mate on e8.

23 Rxc1 Bxc1 24 Bf6 Ra8 25 Rc4 Bxa3 26 Bd4 Bc5!

Black returns the pawn to reach a technically winning endgame.

27 Bxc5 dxc5 28 Rxc5 a3 29 Rc1 a2 White resigns

There is no hope. For example: 30 Ra1 Kf8 31 Kg2 Ke7 32 Kf3 Kd6 33 Kf4 h6 34 Ke4 Ra4+ 35 Kd3 Kxd5 36 Kc3 Ke4 37 Kb3 Ra7 38 Rxa2 Rxa2 39 Kxa2 Kf3 and the black king gobbles up the white pawns.

Game 9
☐ **Malakhov** ■ **Svidler**
Elista 1997

---

1 e4 c5 2 Nf3 d6 3 d4 cxd4 4 Nxd4 Nf6 5 Nc3 Nc6 6 Nde2 g6 7 g3 Bg7 8 Bg2 0-0 9 0-0 Rb8

Preparing queenside counterplay with ...b7-b5.

10 a4 a6 11 Nd5

Occupying this square with the knight is very much normal procedure in the g3 lines.

11...b5

11...Nxd5?! 12 exd5! improves the pawn structure in White's favour. The pawn on d5 is a slight thorn in Black's position and the e7-pawn could eventually become exposed down the half-open e-file.

12 axb5 axb5 13 h3

White wants to play Bc1-e3 without the hassle of having to worry about ...Ng4.

13...b4 14 Be3 Nd7!

Black is ready to eject the knight with ...e7-e6.

15 Qc1

Defending the b2-pawn. Note that after 15 Nd4? Black can win a piece in a surprising way: 15...Bxd4 (Black swaps off his pride and joy but...) 16 Bxd4 e6! 17 Ne3 e5 18 Ba7 Rb7 and the bishop on a7 is trapped.

TIP: Do not dismiss strange looking moves – they may be both strange and good!

15...e6! 16 Ndf4 Qc7 17 Ra2 Nf6 18 Nd3 Rd8 19 c4 Bb7 20 b3 (Diagram 16)

20...Nd7

Here Black could have played 20...Na5!, hitting both the pawn on e4 and the one on b3. Malakhov gives the following line: 21 Nd4 Bxe4 22 Bxe4 Nxe4 23 Nb5 Nxb3! 24 Nxc7 Nxc1 25 Rxc1 b3 with a very unclear position.

21 Rd1 Nce5?

Not good. Black sacrifices his b4-pawn but his calculations are flawed.

22 Nxb4 Nc5 23 Nd4! Bxe4 24 Bxe4 Rxb4

24...Nxe4 allows 25 Na6, forking queen and rook.

25 Nb5! Qb6 26 Qa3 Nxc4?

26...Qb8! 27 Qxb4 Nxe4 was the last chance.

27 bxc4 Rxc4 28 Bd3! Black resigns

28...Qxb5 29 Bxc4 Qxc4 30 Bxc5 and White is a rook ahead for an insignificant two pawns.

Summary

1) The Sicilian Dragon is for brave souls. If White plays the dreaded Yugoslav Attack then both players can look forward to a bloodthirsty battle.

2) White players of a more peaceful nature will be inclined to play either the Classical or the g3 variation.

3) The Levenfish Attack contains lots of early tricks and black players need to memorise a reliable defence against this.

4) The g3 variation is deceptive – it's better than it looks!

Chapter Two

The Najdorf Variation

- The Main Line: 6 Bg5
- The English Attack
- White Plays Be2

1 e4 c5 2 Nf3 d6 3 d4 cxd4 4 Nxd4 Nf6 5 Nc3 a6 (Diagram 1)

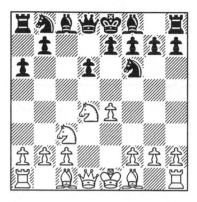

Diagram 1
The starting position for the Najdorf Variation

The Najdorf Variation one of the most ambitious and positionally motivated lines of the Sicilian and, along with the Dragon, also one of
the most popular. Black's little pawn move ...a7-a6 looks at first sight
to be a bit peculiar, but it does have purpose and is also something of
a high-class waiting move. Black waits for White to commit himself
before choosing his pawn structure and development.

In many cases the move ...a7-a6 is simply a precursor to the space
gaining advance ...e7-e5. It should be said that the immediate 5...e5 is
possible, but then 6 Bb5+! is a good reply. After 6...Bd7 7 Bxd7+ Qxd7
the move 8 Nf5 is strong for White.

After 5...a6 standard play by White will be met with ...e7-e5, followed
by consistent development. This may include ...Be7, 0-0, ...Nc6 (or
...Nbd7), ...Be6 (or ...b7-b5 and ...Bb7). Often Black will be looking to
exploit his extra central pawn with the freeing advance ...d7-d5. A
successful advance will usually ensure that Black gains at least
equality, so it's up to White to prevent or dissuade Black from carrying out this plan.

The Najdorf was first utilised by players such as the Czech IM Karel
Opocensky in the 1940s and was later refined by GM Miguel Najdorf,
whose name it then took. At the highest level, the Najdorf is the most
popular of all Sicilians and experts agree that it is 100% sound. It's a
favourite of world champions Bobby Fischer and Garry Kasparov and
is in the armoury of many of today's top players. White players are
constantly looking for new and fruitful ways to battle against the Najdorf and we shall look at the most important systems in this chapter.

One point that should be mentioned here is that there is a strong
similarity between the Najdorf and the Scheveningen (the subject of
Chapter 3) and they often transpose into one another. In general, I've
taken the Najdorf to be lines which include ...e7-e5 and the

Scheveningen to be lines which include ...e7-e6 (with the exception of 6 Bg5 against the Najdorf, when Black's best reply is 6...e6 – see below). The move 6 Bc4, another popular try against the Najdorf, is dealt with in the Scheveningen chapter as Black almost always replies with 6...e6.

The Main Line: 6 Bg5

1 e4 c5 2 Nf3 d6 3 d4 cxd4 4 Nxd4 Nf6 5 Nc3 a6 6 Bg5

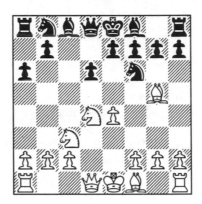

Diagram 2
White plays 6 Bg5

Diagram 3
A typical position in the 6 Bg5 Najdorf

This is probably White's most aggressive attempt against the Najdorf. White develops the c1-bishop onto an attacking square, where it puts immediate pressure on the black knight on f6, one of the key defenders of the crucial d5-square. In this way it is difficult for Black to play in the typical 'Najdorf' way (see the next note).

6...e6

The move 6...e5 would be the characteristic 'Najdorf' way forward, but in this instance it would be a positional error, one which would completely justify White's previous move. After 7 Bxf6 Qxf6 8 Nd5 Qd8 9 Nf5 White has achieved maximum control over the d5-square, with no real concessions that you would find in, say, the Sveshnikov Variation (see Chapter 4). Therefore Black adopts a more restrained 'Scheveningen' pawn structure.

7 f4

White continues to play aggressively and gains more space in the centre. Black now always has to watch out for two central advances: e4-e5 and f4-f5.

7...Be7

A logical move, breaking the pin on the knight and continuing to develop the kingside. However, Black does have some major alternatives here:

a) 7...Qb6 introduces the infamous 'Poisoned Pawn' Variation, in which Black's queen makes a daring snatch of White's b2-pawn (see Game 12).

b) 7...b5!?, an invention of the famous Soviet GM Lev Polugaevsky, is perhaps an even more provocative move for Black, who ignores White's advances in the centre and starts a pawn lunge on the queenside. Opening theory suggests that this line is just about playable but Black really needs to know what he is doing! One point is that after 8 e5 dxe5 9 fxe5 Qc7! 10 exf6 Black regains his piece with 10...Qe5+.

8 Qf3

White prepares for queenside castling as he will want to launch his pawns forward on the kingside.

TIP: If you plan to launch your pawns forward on one wing, it usually makes sense to castle on the other wing.

8...Qc7

Of course Black can castle but in this particular line it makes more sense to delay this and begin queenside operations immediately.

9 0-0-0 Nbd7 10 g4

White begins the pawn assault on the kingside.

10...b5

Likewise, Black starts counterplay on the queenside.

11 Bxf6

White's bishop was actually beginning to get in the way on g5, so White saves time by exchanging it.

11...Nxf6

The most common, although 11...Bxf6 and 11...gxf6!? are playable.

12 g5

White gains further time for his assault on the kingside by attacking the black knight.

Exercise 2: What's wrong with the move 12 e5, which attacks both the f6-knight and the a8-rook?

12...Nd7 (Diagram 3)

Strategies

White will continue to march forward with his pawns on the kingside, looking to open lines of attack against the enemy king. One advance worth noting is f4-f5, which puts pressure on the e6-pawn, the only defender of the crucial d5-square. If this square falls in to White hands, then this could spell trouble for Black. The downside of the f4-f5 advance is that it gives Black possession of the e5-square. We've already learnt that this is a very useful square for a black knight.

In special circumstances White can consider breaking through with piece sacrifices on e6 and b5 and these possibilities must always be taken into consideration by both players.

Once again Black's counterplay is on the queenside. If White continues with no plan, then Black can proceed by dislodging the c3-knight with ...b5-b4, followed by an attack on the slightly vulnerable e4-pawn with ...Bb7 and ...Nc5. Black can increase the pressure further with ...Ra8-c8, after which the queen and rook hit the c2-pawn in front of the white king. Black will often delay castling kingside in favour of starting immediate queenside action.

Theoretical?

The main line 6 Bg5 is probably the most theoretical line of the Najdorf and black players certainly need to remember a few key lines, particularly if he wants to take on the complexities of the Poisoned Pawn Variation. However, unlike in the Yugoslav Attack against the Dragon, Black is likely to have some success by simply playing to the position's strategic demands as White does not have such a straight-forward plan of a mating attack.

Statistics

6 Bg5 has traditionally been considered as the 'main line' of the Najdorf but things have changed over the last few years. A survey of *The Week in Chess* (a database of over 300,000 games from 1994-2002) shows that 6 Bg5 is now only White's third most popular response to the Najdorf, behind both the English Attack (6 Be3) and the classical 6 Be2. This database also revealed only a 48% score for White, although on average the white players were rated slightly lower than the black players.

Illustrative Games

Game 10
□ **Relange** ■ **Sadler**
Hastings 1997/98

1 e4 c5 2 Nf3 d6 3 d4 cxd4 4 Nxd4 Nf6 5 Nc3 a6 6 Bg5 e6 7 f4 Be7 8 Qf3 Qc7 9 0-0-0 Nbd7 10 g4 b5 11 Bxf6 Nxf6 12 g5 Nd7 13 f5!

White lunges further forward on the kingside. On first sight this looks a little premature as Black can now capture a pawn with check, but in fact 13 f5 is White's most common move. Giving up the pawn opens lines on the kingside, which White can use to attack the black king. If White doesn't want to give up a pawn he can continue with 13 h4, supporting the g5-pawn and preparing f4-f5. Of course, this uses an extra tempo and allows Black to continue his counterplay with 13...b4.

 NOTE: In sharp lines, where the gain or the loss of a tempo can be crucial, holding onto a pawn may be of secondary importance.

13...Bxg5+

Accepting the pawn offer must be the critical test, but Black can also play 13...Nc5 (see Game 11).

14 Kb1 Ne5

As we have seen before, the e5-square is often a good defensive outpost for Black in the Sicilian.

15 Qh5

By attacking the bishop on g5 and also pinning the f7-pawn, White immediately regains his sacrificed pawn.

15...Qd8 (Diagram 4)

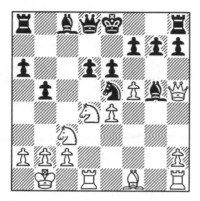

Diagram 4
White can regain his pawn

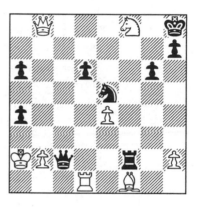

Diagram 5
What does Black have up his sleeve?

16 Nxe6!

The point of White's previous move.

16...Bxe6 17 fxe6 0-0

It seems that Black is risking a lot by castling into so many open lines, but his position remains extremely resourceful.

18 Rg1 Bf6 19 exf7+ Kh8!

The immediate 19...Rxf7 20 Bh3! leaves Black threatened with Be6, so Black recaptures the f-pawn in his own time.

20 Nd5 g6 21 Qh3 Rxf7 22 Nf4 Qd7 23 Qb3

White decides to keep the queens on the board, but perhaps this was not wise. 23 Qxd7 Nxd7 24 Nd5 Be5 leads to a roughly level ending.

23...Qc6 24 Bh3 Bg7 25 Rgf1 Raf8 26 Ne6 Rxf1 27 Bxf1 Rf2

Black's king is safely tucked away on h8 and, if anything, it's Black who is more active.

28 a4? bxa4!

It says something about modern chess when a 'novelty' is played on move twenty-eight! English GM Matthew Sadler had reached the same position a few months earlier against the late Estonian Grandmaster Lembit Oll. On that occasion he had played the inferior 28...b4, eventually losing the game. In all likelihood, Relange was simply following Oll's play and analysis, but he was in for an almighty shock!

WARNING: Always carefully check published analysis. That includes the analysis in this book!

29 Qb8+ Bf8

The only move.

30 Nxf8 Qxc2+ 31 Ka2 (Diagram 5)

31...Nc6!!

This was the real surprise. Oll's analysis had just given Black regaining his piece with 31...Qb3+ 32 Qxb3 axb3+ 33 Kxb3 Rxf8 34 Bxa6, when White's passed b-pawn gives him the edge in the ending.

Sadler's move attacks the white queen but allows a double check. However, this doesn't help White.

32 Nxg6+ Kg7 33 Qb7+

After either 33 Qc7+ Kh6! or 33 Qh8+ Kh6 White cannot deal with the threats on the queenside, for example: 34 Rb1 Nb4+ 35 Ka1 Qxb1+! 36 Kxb1 Rxf1 mate.

33...Rf7! 34 Qb6 a5! White resigns

Despite being a piece up, White is totally lost, for example:

a) 35 Rb1 Nb4+ 36 Ka1 Qxb1+! 37 Kxb1 Rxf1 mate. We've already seen this mating motif.

b) 35 Re1 Nb4+ 36 Ka1 Qd2 37 Rb1 a3 38 Bc4 axb2+ 39 Rxb2 Qc1+ 40 Rb1 Qa3+ 41 Ba2 Qxa2 mate.

Game 11
□ **Lobron** ■ **Chandler**
German Bundesliga 1986

---

1 e4 c5 2 Nf3 d6 3 d4 cxd4 4 Nxd4 Nf6 5 Nc3 a6 6 Bg5 e6 7 f4 Be7 8 Qf3 Qc7 9 0-0-0 Nbd7 10 g4 b5 11 Bxf6 Nxf6 12 g5 Nd7 13 f5 Nc5

By not capturing the pawn on g5, Black tries to keep the kingside as closed as possible.

14 f6

Forcing the black bishop back to its original square.

14...gxf6 15 gxf6 Bf8 16 Rg1

A very natural move. The rook occupies the only open file on the board. Black seems to have the crucial entry points covered, or does he?

16...Bd7 (Diagram 6)

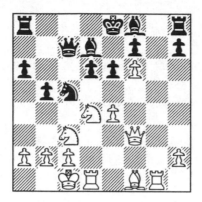

Diagram 6
How does White continue?

Diagram 7
Nf6+ is looming

17 Rg7!

An unpleasant move for Black to meet. He could ignore the rook but then it's difficult to castle queenside without losing a crucial pawn on f7. In this game Black chooses to capture although this does leave White with an impressive looking passed pawn only one square from promotion.

17...Bxg7 18 fxg7 Rg8 19 e5

Uncovering an attack on the a8-rook.

19...d5?

It seems natural to block the attack in this way, but in fact now Black is in big trouble. Correct is 19...0-0-0! 20 exd6 Qb7!, after which the game remains very unclear.

20 Qf6!

Now Black has substantial problems with his king.

20...b4

Or 20...Qd8 21 b4! Na4 22 Nxa4 bxa4 23 Bd3! and White has a major threat of Bxh7. Note that 23...Qxf6 24 exf6, protecting the g7-pawn, doesn't help Black at all.

21 Nf5!

After this sacrifice White breaks through Black's defences.

21...exf5 22 Nxd5 Qd8 23 Qd6 (Diagram 7)

Threatening Nf6+.

23...f6

Or 23...Ne4 24 Nf6+! Nxf6 25 exf6 and Black is totally busted, e.g. 25...Ra7 26 Re1+ Be6 27 Rxe6+! fxe6 28 Qxe6+ Re7 29 f7 mate!

24 Bc4! Be6 25 Nc7+ Kf7 26 Bxe6+ Black resigns

After 26...Kxg7 27 Qxc5 White wins easily.

Game 12
□ Timman ■ Ljubojevic
Linares 1985

1 e4 c5 2 Nf3 d6 3 d4 cxd4 4 Nxd4 Nf6 5 Nc3 a6 6 Bg5 e6 7 f4 Qb6

Black enters the Poisoned Pawn Variation.

8 Qd2

If White is scared of sacrificing his b-pawn then he can play something like 8 Nb3 but this promises no theoretical advantage and the majority of white players feel up to the challenge of gambiting a pawn.

8...Qxb2!

There is no going back now, otherwise there would be no real point to 8...Qb6. With this move Black grabs a hot pawn. However, by doing so, Black firmly passes the initiative over to White and falls behind in development. Black's queen can be of nuisance value, but Black must also watch out that his queen doesn't get trapped deep in enemy territory (even Bobby Fischer got his trapped in a World Championship clash with Boris Spassky!).

On the other hand, a pawn is a pawn! The onus is on White to prove that he has something concrete for his investment. Slow play by White will simply allow Black to catch up in development.

The Poisoned Pawn has received a thumbs up from many grandmasters and has been a long time favourite of world champions Kasparov and Fischer. Black scores a very healthy 52% in *Mega Database 2002*, although this figure is tempered by the fact that often higher rated players choose this risky line when playing for a win against lower rated players.

9 Rb1 Qa3 10 Be2

Continuing to develop and preparing to castle kingside. As you would expect in such a complex line, White has many other playable alternatives, such as 10 e5, 10 f5 and 10 Bxf6.

10...Be7 11 0-0 Nbd7 (Diagram 8) 12 e5!?

In for a penny, in for a pound. With this move White offers more material in an attempt to blow open the position before Black has time to catch up in development.

NOTE: After an initial sacrifice, further material is often invested in order to keep the attack going.

12...dxe5 13 fxe5 Nxe5 14 Bxf6 Bxf6

Theory prefers 14...gxf6!, for example: 15 Ne4 f5 16 Rb3 Qa4 17 Nxf5!? with massive complications. However, this is certainly something that black players would need to know before commencing battle. 14...Bxf6 looks perfectly normal, after all.

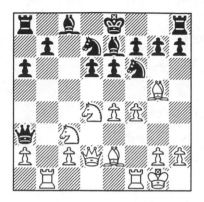

Diagram 8
In for a penny...

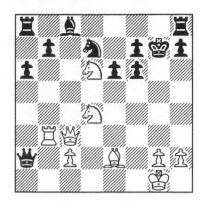

Diagram 9
White to play and win!

15 Rxf6!

Adding more fuel to the fire. White has gone passed caring how much he has to sacrifice in order to get at Black's king.

15...gxf6 16 Ne4 Nd7?

16...Qe7 is a stronger defence. Now White's attack begins to assume menacing proportions.

17 Rb3 Qxa2

After 17...Qe7 Black seems to have everything covered, but White can play 18 Nc6!! bxc6 19 Nd6+ and Black's in big trouble. For example: 19...Kf8? 20 Qh6+ Kg8 21 Rg3 mate; or 19...Kd8 20 Qa5+ Nb6 21 Qxb6+ Kd7 22 Ne4 and White has an awesome attack.

18 Nd6+ Kf8 19 Qc3

Threatening, amongst other things, simply Nxc8.

19...Kg7 (Diagram 9)

20 N4f5+! exf5 21 Nxf5+ Kg6

Or 21...Kf8 22 Qb4+ Ke8 23 Qe7 mate.

22 Qh3 Black resigns

There is no good defence to the threat of Rg3. For example: 22...h5 (22...Qa1+ 23 Kf2 only delays matters) 23 Rg3+ Kh7 24 Qxh5 mate.

The English Attack

1 e4 c5 2 Nf3 d6 3 d4 cxd4 4 Nxd4 Nf6 5 Nc3 a6 6 Be3 (Diagram 10)

This move signals White's intentions of playing the English Attack, so called because of its development and utilisation by top English grandmasters such as John Nunn, Nigel Short and Murray Chandler in the 1980s. This system of development is effective against both the

Najdorf and the Scheveningen (see Chapter 3).

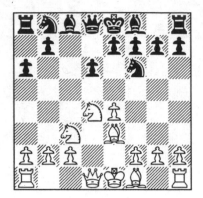

Diagram 10	**Diagram 11**
The English Attack	A typical position in the English Attack

6...e5

Black replies in typical Najdorf style. The move 6...e6 would transpose into the Scheveningen (see Chapter 3), while the 'spoiling' idea of 6...Ng4 is dealt with in Game 15.

7 Nb3

The aggressive 7 Nf5 is premature. Black obtains a free game after either 7...Bxf5 8 exf5 d5! or simply 7...d5!.

It should be said that 7 Nf3 is also playable, but 7 Nb3 is more popular and far more dangerous for Black.

7...Be6

Black simply begins to develop his pieces.

8 f3

An important move for the English Attack. As with the Yugoslav Attack in the Dragon, White prepares Qd2, and 0-0-0, together with a launch of the kingside pawns. The move f2-f3 both prevents an annoying ...Ng4 and supports the advance g2-g4.

See below for the statistics on this position.

8...Nbd7 9 g4

An important space gaining move on the kingside. The positional motivation behind the idea is that White intends g4-g5, forcing the black knight to move away from its ideal posting at f6 and lessening Black's control over the d5-square.

White can also delay this advance and continue development with 9 Qd2 (see Game 13).

NOTE: Control of the d5-square is of utmost importance in the Najdorf Sicilian.

9...b5 (Diagram 11)

We've seen this typical lunge on the queenside before. Black initiates counterplay on the queenside.

Strategies

The stage is set for another uncompromising battle between the two sides. White will develop with Qd2 and 0-0-0 and, if allowed, will push forward on the kingside with g4-g5. Black may forestall this advance with the defensive move ...h7-h6, or be ready to move his knight to either h5 or d7 (once the other knight has vacated this square). If the f6-knight is forced to move elsewhere (g8, for example) then this is usually a sign that things have gone wrong for Black.

Once again Black's counterplay lies very much on the queenside. Often, in the fight for control over the crucial d5-square, Black plays the pawn lunge ...b5-b4. This asks the question of the knight on c3, which will either jump into d5 or retreat elsewhere. Black will find it difficult to arrange the freeing advance ...d6-d5, but if White is careless enough to allow this, then this often turns out to be favourable for Black.

In general, play is sharp and dynamic, often involving positional or tactical sacrifices from both sides.

Theoretical?

The English Attack is a relatively new system and as such there is less theory to learn than, say, the 6 Bg5 Najdorf. Although the battle can be extremely sharp, more often than not, playing by general principles should be enough for a reasonable level of success.

Statistics

According to *The Week in Chess*, 6 Be3 is currently the most popular choice against the Najdorf, just slightly more so than the classical 6 Be2. It's a favourite of Kasparov, Anand, Shirov and Adams, to name but a few top class grandmasters.

Using the larger *Mega Database 2002*, I found over a thousand examples of the position arising after 8 f3. White scores 53%, while 70% of the games are decisive.

Illustrative Games

Game 13
□ **Morozevich** ■ **Ftacnik**
German Bundesliga 1998

1 e4 c5 2 Nf3 d6 3 d4 cxd4 4 Nxd4 Nf6 5 Nc3 a6 6 f3

An unusual move order, which is becoming more popular. This has the advantage of cutting out Black's option of 6...Ng4 (see Game 15).

6...e5

If Black wants to 'punish' White for his move order, then he could try either 6...Nc6 or 6...Qb6, both putting early pressure on d4.

7 Nb3 Be6 8 Be3

Now we are back in the main line.

8...Nbd7 9 Qd2 Be7

A major alternative here is 9...b5!? 10 g4 Nb6, clearing space on d7 so that 11 g5 can be met with 11...Nfd7.

10 g4 h6

This move buys Black a bit of time as it dissuades White from playing g4-g5 for the moment.

11 0-0-0 b5 12 h4

Lending extra support for the g4-g5 push.

12...Nb6 13 Qf2 Rb8 14 Nc5!?

Making use of the pin on the d-file in order to activate the knight.

14...Bc8 15 Be2

Connecting the rooks and preparing the g4-g5 lunge.

In his notes to the game, Morozevich gives as an alternative the mind-boggling variation 15 g5!? hxg5 16 hxg5 Rxh1 17 gxf6 Rxf1! (17...Bxf6 18 Bxb5+ axb5 19 Rxh1 is favourable for White) 18 fxg7 Rxf2 19 g8Q+ Bf8 20 Bxf2 b4! 21 Ne2 Qf6 and Black is fine!

15...Qc7

Perhaps Black should have continued queenside operations with 15...b4!?, forcing the white knight to retreat.

16 g5 dxc5

The move 16...hxg5 shows a negative point of 10...h6. After 17 hxg5 Rxh1 18 Rxh1 it's White who is in possession of the open h-file.

17 gxf6 gxf6 18 f4! (Diagram 12)

White is a pawn down, but more importantly Black's king has no safe haven. This headache stays with Black for the rest of the game.

18...b4 19 Nd5 Nxd5 20 exd5! e4 21 f5 Bd6 22 Qg2 Bd7!? 23 Bh5!

Targeting the weak f7-pawn, so often the Achilles' heel in Black's position.

23...Rf8

23...c4 loses to 24 Bxf7+! Kxf7 25 Qg6+ Ke7 26 Qg7+ and Qxh8.

24 Rhe1 Bxf5 25 Rf1 Qd7 26 Qg7!

The f6-pawn falls and Black's position is on the point of collapse.

26...Bh3 27 Rxf6 Qe7 28 Qxh6 Be5 29 Re6!

This temporary sacrifice is a killer. In the long run Black is forced to lose material.

29...Bxe6 30 dxe6 Qf6 31 exf7+ Rxf7 32 Bxf7+ Kxf7 33 Qh7+ Ke8 34 Qg8+ Qf8 35 Qe6+ Qe7 36 Qc6+ Kf7 37 Rd7 **Black resigns**

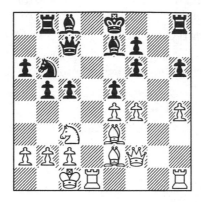

Diagram 12
Where is the black king going?

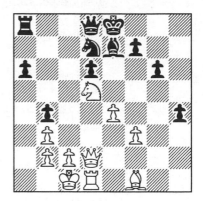

Diagram 13
White is ready to attack

Game 14
□ **Adams** ■ **Svidler**
Dos Hermanas 1999

1 e4 c5 2 Nf3 d6 3 d4 cxd4 4 Nxd4 Nf6 5 Nc3 a6 6 Be3 e5 7 Nb3 Be6 8 f3 Nbd7 9 g4 b5 10 g5 b4

Black responds to the attack on his king's knight with one of his own on the c3-knight. This is not an uncommon idea in the Sicilian. 10...Nh5 is a sensible alternative.

11 Ne2

11 Nd5 is another common move. After 11...Nxd5 12 exd5 Bf5 13 Bd3 Bxd3 14 Qxd3 Black continues with ...Be7 and ...0-0.

11...Nh5 12 Qd2 Be7

Preparing to castle, but Black should also consider delaying this in favour of 12...a5, counter-attacking on the queenside.

13 Ng3

Challenging the black knight on h5.

White can grab a hot pawn with 13 Qxb4 Bxg5 14 Bxg5 Qxg5 15 Qxd6 but after 15...Rd8 Black already has a dangerous threat of 16...Qh4+.

13...Nf4

13...Nxg3? 14 hxg3 gives White an excellent half-open h-file down which to attack.

 WARNING: Be careful not to gift your opponent with an avenue of attack.

14 h4

Protecting the g5-pawn.

14...h6!?

Black fights back on the kingside. Note that this is an advantage of delaying castling. This wouldn't have been possible if Black had already committed his king to this side of the board.

15 Bxf4 exf4 16 Nh5 Bxb3 17 axb3 g6 18 Nxf4 hxg5 19 Nd5 Rxh4?

A mistake according to Adams. Black should have played either 19...gxh4 or 19...g4!?.

20 Rxh4 gxh4 21 0-0-0 (Diagram 13)

Now White is well co-ordinated and his attack is worth more than the pawn deficit.

21...Nf6 22 Bc4 Nxd5

22...a5 is answered by 23 Qh6!, planning to meet 23...Nxd5 with the decisive 24 Bb5+ (Svidler).

23 Qxd5 Bg5+ 24 Kb1 Ra7 25 e5! Kf8

Or 25...Rd7 26 e6! and White crashes through on the weakened light squares, for example: 26...fxe6 27 Qxe6+ Qe7 28 Qg8+ Qf8 29 Qxg6+ and Qxg5.

26 e6!

This is even stronger than 26 exd6.

26...Bf6

After 26...fxe6 27 Qxe6 Rg7 28 Rxd6 Black cannot hope to survive the onslaught.

27 exf7 Qe7 28 f4!

Preventing ...Qe5, which would otherwise force an exchange of queens.

28...Qxf7 29 Qxd6+ Qe7 30 Qb8+ Kg7 31 Rg1

Now White targets the g6-pawn and there is no defence.

31...Kh6 32 Bd3! Rd7 33 Qg8 Black resigns

The g6-pawn falls and Black is soon mated.

Game 15
□ **Shirov** ■ **Kasparov**
Linares 1997

---

1 e4 c5 2 Nf3 d6 3 d4 cxd4 4 Nxd4 Nf6 5 Nc3 a6 6 Be3 Ng4

Note that Black's fifth move means that there is no Bb5+, otherwise 6...Ng4 would simply lose material.

7 Bg5

White wants to keep his dark-squared bishop. The price for this is that Black gains time by attacking the bishop while also continuing to develop.

7...h6 8 Bh4 g5 9 Bg3 Bg7

The position now resembles a Dragon rather than a Najdorf. Black is well developed, but White can hope that the g5-h6 structure can be attacked later on.

10 Be2 h5 11 Bxg4

White decides to get rid of the troublesome knight. Alternatives include striking back on the kingside with 11 h4.

11...Bxg4

More recently Kasparov has played 11...hxg4!?, opening up the h-file for the rook.

12 f3 Bd7 13 0-0 Nc6 14 Bf2 e6!?

This double-edged move was Kasparov's invention. On the one hand, Black prevents White from playing Nd5 but, on the other, the d6-pawn is now devoid of protection and could become a target.

15 Nce2

It was later discovered that 15 Nde2!, immediately hitting the d6-pawn, is more dangerous for Black.

15...Ne5 16 b3 (Diagram 14)

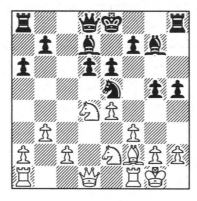

Diagram 14
Black plays with purpose

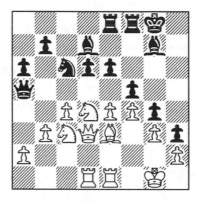

Diagram 15
Time for action in the centre

16...g4

Typical Kasparov aggression. Black gains useful space on the kingside.

17 f4 h4! 18 Be3

Black can afford to leave the knight hanging on e5. After 18 fxe5 dxe5 the white knight has no place to go and Black regains the piece.

18...h3 19 g3 Nc6 20 Qd3 0-0 21 Rad1 f5!

Black continues his kingside offensive.

22 c4

Or 22 Nxc6 Bxc6 23 exf5 exf5 24 Qxd6 Qe8 and suddenly Black has a nasty threat of ...Qe4, intending ...Qg2 mate.

22...Qa5 23 Nc3?

A mistake, according to Kasparov. White should offer the exchange of queens with 23 Qd2!.

23...Rae8 24 Rfe1? (Diagram 15)

And here 24 Nde2 was stronger.

24...e5!

Kasparov blasts open the centre to his advantage.

25 Nxc6 Bxc6 26 b4 Qa3 27 b5 exf4 28 Bxf4 axb5 29 cxb5 Qc5+ 30 Be3?

White's only chance to stay in the game was with 30 Re3!.

30...Qxc3 31 bxc6 Qxc6

Black is a pawn up with a good position. Kasparov doesn't slip up from here.

32 Qxd6 Qxe4 33 Qd5+ Qxd5 34 Rxd5 Bc3 35 Re2 Re4 36 Kf2 Rfe8 37 Rd3 Bf6 38 Red2 Rxe3! White resigns

Black wins after 39 Rxe3 Rxe3 40 Kxe3 Bg5+ 41 Ke2 Bxd2 42 Kxd2 f4! 43 gxf4 g3! 44 hxg3 h2 and the pawn promotes.

White Plays Be2

1 e4 c5 2 Nf3 d6 3 d4 cxd4 4 Nxd4 Nf6 5 Nc3 a6 6 Be2 (Diagram 16)

White develops classically and gives a clear indication that he will castle on the kingside.

6...e5

The move 6...e6 would transpose into the Scheveningen (see Chapter 3).

7 Nb3

7 Nf5 may be the first and most aggressive move that springs to mind, but this is hardly ever played. The reason being that it allows Black to strike immediately in the centre with 7...d5!, exploiting the vulnerable nature of the knight on f5. Now 8 Nxd5 Nxd5 9 Qxd5 Qxd5 10 exd5 Bxf5 wins a piece, so White should continue 8 Bg5 d4 9 Bxf6 Qxf6 10 Nd5 Qd8. Superficially, White looks well placed, but Black's advance in the centre has given him space for his bishops and the knight on f5 will be forced back with ...g7-g6.

7 Nf3 is playable but is seen much less often than 7 Nb3, perhaps because white players are reluctant to block their f2-pawn, which advances to f3 or f4 in many lines.

7...Be7

Black sensibly continues to develop his kingside and prepares to castle.

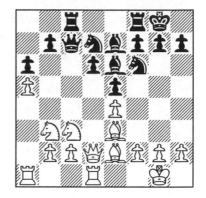

Diagram 16	Diagram 17
White plays 6 Be2	A typical position arising from 6 Be2

8 0-0 0-0 9 Be3

White has quite a few different plans here but I will concentrate on one of the most logical ones. Traditionally, this bishop move is the most common idea, although recently many grandmasters have been paying close attention to the semi-waiting move 9 Kh1 (see Game 17). Other ideas for White include the aggressive pawn advance 9 f4.

9...Be6

A good place for the bishop, supporting the desired ...d6-d5 advance and controlling the c4-square. Another way for Black to develop his bishop would be with ...b7-b5 and ...Bb7. Here, however, 9...b5 would be a little premature due to 10 Nd5! and if 10...Nxd5?, then 11 Qxd5 wins material! White also wins material after 10...Nxe4? 11 Bf3 f5 12 Nxe7+ Qxe7 13 Qd5+.

 TIP: Both players should be wary of Nc3-d5 ideas for White.

10 Qd2

More sensible stuff. White prepares to add pressure along the half-open d-file by placing a rook on d1.

10...Nbd7

It's actually possible for Black to play the freeing advance 10...d5!? now, but he prefers to develop fully before trying to carry out the advance. After 11 exd5 Nxd5 12 Nxd5 Qxd5 13 Qxd5 Bxd5 14 Rfd1 Bc6 15 Na5 White is better developed and keeps an edge.

11 a4

A good move, preventing Black from gaining space with ...b7-b5.

11...Rc8 12 a5

Further restriction. This move prevents the knight from using the b6-square and prepares to meet ...b7-b5 with capturing en passant, leaving an isolated and vulnerable a6-pawn.

12...Qc7

Vacating the d8-square, which may be used by the f8-rook.

13 Rfd1 (Diagram 17)

Further pressure along the d-file. Here White uses the f1-rook to go to d1 as the a1-rook is already doing a job on the a-file and may even enter the game via a4.

We are following the game Karpov-Nunn, Amsterdam 1985 (see Game 16).

Strategies

Play is certainly more positional than tactical in nature and it's quite rare for either side to go for an all-out attack on the opponent's king. If we take a starting position to be after 8...0-0, then it's possible to say that both White and Black have a number of different ideas and piece deployments. However, one constant theme remains throughout: the fight for control over the d5-square. Whoever wins this battle is likely to be successful overall.

Theoretical?

6 Be2 is the least theoretical line of the Najdorf and can be virtually played on general principles alone. It's certainly more important to understand the various ideas associated with either side.

Statistics

According to *The Week in Chess*, 6 Be2 is comes a very close second in the popularity stakes to the English Attack. Given its strategical nature, 6 Be2 appeals more to quiet and positional players. However, I found over 5,000 games with 6 Be2 e5 in *Mega Database 2002*, and the results are surprisingly good for Black, who scores an excellent 52%. This implies that 6 Be2 is not a particularly dangerous system.

Illustrative Games

Game 16
☐ **Karpov** ■ **Nunn**
Amsterdam 1985

1 e4 c5 2 Nf3 d6 3 d4 Nf6 4 Nc3 cxd4 5 Nxd4 a6 6 Be2 e5 7 Nb3 Be7 8 0-0 0-0 9 Be3 Be6 10 Qd2 Nbd7 11 a4 Rc8 12 a5 Qc7 13 Rfd1 Rfd8

Karpov's exemplary treatment in this well-known game cast doubts upon this natural-looking move and forced black players to look at other options such as 13...Nc5, for example: 14 Nxc5 dxc5 15 f3 Rfd8 16 Qe1 Rxd1 17 Qxd1 c4 18 Na4 Bb4 19 Bb6 Qc6 20 c3 Be7 with a level position, Brunner-Gallagher, Biel 1990.

14 Qe1 Qc6

Preparing ...d6-d5, which White's next move prevents.

15 Bf3 Bc4 (Diagram 18)

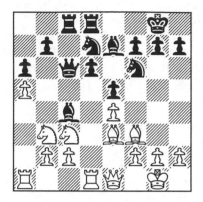
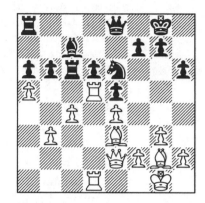

Diagram 18	Diagram 19
White has a good plan available	Black's c6-rook is lacking squares

16 Nc1!

Terrific positional play from Karpov. He takes his worst-placed minor piece and manoeuvres it so that it plays a crucial role in the battle for the d5-square.

TIP: In quiet positions it is often a good idea to re-deploy your worst placed piece.

16...h6 17 N1a2

The knight is coming to b4. Black now has no chance of completing the ...d6-d5 break and is condemned to a long and passive defence.

17...Nc5 18 Nb4 Qe8 19 g3 Rc7 20 Bg2 Rdc8 21 b3 Be6 22 Ncd5

White has total dominance of the d5-square, which he now uses as an effective outpost.

22...Nxd5 23 Nxd5 Bxd5 24 Rxd5 Rc6 25 Rad1 Ne6 26 c4 Bg5 27 Ba7 Ra8 28 Bb6 Bd8 29 Be3 Bc7 30 Qe2 b6 (Diagram 19) 31 b4!

This wins material.

31...bxa5 32 b5 axb5 33 cxb5 Rc5 34 Bxc5 Nxc5 35 Bf1 a4 36 Qc2 a3 37 Bc4 Ne6 38 R5d3 Nd4 39 Qa2 Bb6 40 Rxa3 1-0

Here Black lost on time, but his position was hopeless in any case. A marvellous positional display from Karpov.

Game 17
☐ **Rohl** ■ **Leitao**
San Felipe 1998

---

1 e4 c5 2 Nf3 d6 3 d4 cxd4 4 Nxd4 Nf6 5 Nc3 a6 6 Be2 e5 7 Nb3 Be7 8 0-0 0-0 9 Kh1

This non-committal move has become quite trendy in recent years after its successful employment by Garry Kasparov. As we've seen before, the white king is slightly safer on h1, especially if White intends moving his f-pawn up the board. After 9 Kh1 White keeps his options very much open. For example, if Black plays 9...Be6, White can reply with 10 f4!, threatening to force the bishop off this important diagonal with f4-f5. Similarly, if Black plays 9...b5, White can strike at the queenside with 10 a4. Note that 10...b4 11 Nd5 Nxe4 12 Bf3 is winning for White: 12...f5 13 Bxe4 fxe4 14 Nxe7+ Qxe7 15 Qd5+, or 12...Bf5 13 Qe2 Nf6 14 Nxf6+ Bxf6 15 Bxa8.

9...Nbd7

Black's reply is also non-committal. Now ...Be6 is impossible, so Black chooses another development plan.

10 a4 b6!

The bishop is bound for b7, where it both attacks the e4-pawn and supports the ...d7-d5 advance.

11 Be3 Bb7 12 f3

White solidly supports the e4-pawn.

12...Rc8 13 Rf2!

Both sides now concentrate on the main issue: the control of the crucial d5-square.

13...Rc7!

A very clever move, allowing Black to fight for control over d5 with ...Qa8.

14 Bf1

Planning Rf2-d2.

14...Qa8 15 Rd2 h6 16 Nc1 (Diagram 20)

Starting the same manoeuvre as we saw in the previous game. White plans Nc1-a2-b4, with total dominance of the d5-square. Black's solution to this problem is both radical and good.

16...Rxc3!

Another typical ...Rxc3 exchange sacrifice in the Sicilian. Black ruins White's pawn structure on the queenside and eliminates a defender of the d5-square, allowing him to push through with the thematic ...d6-d5 advance.

17 bxc3 d5 18 c4 dxe4!?

Giving up more material in order to start a direct attack against the white king. Also possible is simply 18...d4, after which Black has plenty of compensation in the form of active pieces and weak white pawns.

19 Rxd7 Nxd7 20 Qxd7 exf3 21 Kg1 fxg2 22 Be2 Bf6 23 Qg4 Be7 24 Qd7 Bf6 25 Qg4 Be7 26 Qd7 Bh4!

After a repetition of moves Black hits upon the right idea.

27 Qg4?

According to Leitao, 27 Nd3! offers a better chance of defence.

27...Qd8! 28 Bxh6? (Diagram 21) 28...g5!!

A fabulous move, threatening to mow down the white queen with an avalanche of pawn moves.

29 Bf3

Or 29 Bxf8 f5 and Black will follow up with a decisive ...Qd4+.

29...f5 30 Bxg5

30 Qxg2 loses after 30...Qd4+ 31 Kh1 Qxa1 32 Bxb7 Qxc1+.

30...fxg4 31 Bxd8 Rxf3 White resigns

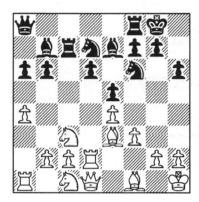

Diagram 20
Black has a radical solution in mind

Diagram 21
How does Black deal with the threat?

Summary

1) The Najdorf is an ideal weapon for ambitious players who are not frightened of learning opening theory.

2) Traditionally, 6 Bg5 has been the most aggressive and theoretical response to the Najdorf. One of Black's responses to this is the notorious Poisoned Pawn Variation, a favourite of both Bobby Fischer and Garry Kasparov.

3) The English Attack is a relatively fresh system which is less complex but just as aggressive as 6 Bg5.

4) White players looking for a quieter life will find that 6 Be2 should suit them.

Chapter Three

The Scheveningen Variation

1 e4 c5 2 Nf3 d6 3 d4 cxd4 4 Nxd4 Nf6 5 Nc3 e6 (Diagram 1)

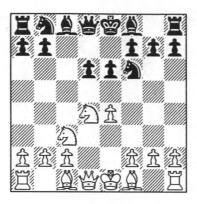

Diagram 1
The Sicilian Scheveningen

This variation of the Sicilian doesn't owe its name to any particular player, rather a town in Holland where the opening was first played in 1923. The main feature of this defence is the 'small centre' that Black possesses: the pawns on e6 and d6. This pair controls many crucial squares in the centre and forms a formidable defensive wall, upon which many overzealous white attacks have been rebuffed. Black plans classical development with ...Be7, ...0-0, ...Nc6 (or possibly ...Nbd7) and the typical queenside counterplay with ...a7-a6 and ...b7-b5. As in the Najdorf, Black is always on the lookout to play a favourable ...d6-d5, liberating his position. White has many aggressive attempts to break down Black's super-solid structure and we will be taking a look at the most important ones in this chapter.

One of the main attractions of the Scheveningen Variation is that Black creates no unnecessary pawn weakness and so his structure is basically sound. Garry Kasparov used the Scheveningen to great effect when he defeated Karpov in their 1985 World Championship Match. Try as he might, Karpov could find no way through the black defences and in the end he even gave up playing 1 e4 against Kasparov.

The Keres Attack

1 e4 c5 2 Nf3 d6 3 d4 cxd4 4 Nxd4 Nf6 5 Nc3 e6 6 g4 (Diagram 2)

The Keres Attack is without doubt the most aggressive way to meet the Scheveningen and is a crucial test of the defence's viability. We've already seen the value of the g2-g4 lunge in the Sicilian and the only difference on this occasion is that White plays it as early as move six. The idea is very straightforward: White wishes to dislodge Black's defensive knight from its favourite f6-post and claim as much space on the kingside as possible.

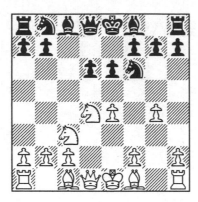

Diagram 2
The Keres Attack

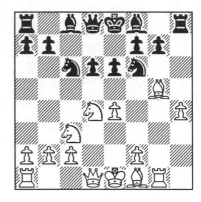

Diagram 3
A typical position from the Keres

6...h6

The most popular response to the Keres Attack. With this move Black stabilises the position of his f6-knight, at least for the moment. It will now take White two more moves to prepare to dislodge it again.

The move 6...d5 is, in a way, logical as it meets the well-known requirement of 'responding to an attack on the wing by a counter-attack in the centre'. However, it also commits the 'sin' of moving a piece (or in this case a pawn) twice in the opening. This loss of time is the most important factor and it's White who comes out on top. For example: 7 exd5 Nxd5 8 Bb5+ Bd7 9 Nxd5 exd5 10 Qe2+ Qe7 11 Be3 g6 12 Bxd7+ Nxd7 13 Nb5 Ne5 14 0-0-0 and White was very well placed in Fischer-Reshevsky, New York 1967.

For the natural developing move 6...Nc6, see Game 19.

7 h4

More aggression. White continues to prepare the g4-g5 advance.

7...Nc6

Sensibly developing another piece.

8 Rg1

This looks a little strange to begin with, but White's play is perfectly logical. The immediate 8 g5 is met by 8...hxg5! and the pin on the h-file prevents White from recapturing with the pawn. After 8 Rg1 White can now recapture with the h-pawn so the g4-g5 push carries more weight. Of course, White can no longer castle on the kingside, but given that he has already launched his kingside pawns forward, he was always intending on castling on the other wing.

8...h5!

Black fights back on the kingside. The idea is that after g4-g5 Black can hop his knight into the g4-square. The move 8...h5 is by far Black's most popular choice.

9 gxh5

White changes plan slightly and gives his g1-rook a half-open g-file.

9...Nxh5 10 Bg5 Nf6 (Diagram 3)

Strategies

White has already achieved quite a bit on the kingside; the rook on g1 is on a half-open file and the bishop on g5 is actively placed. White should be looking to complete development and castle queenside before commencing active duties.

With the kingside so open, Black very rarely castles on that side. Instead, he develops his queenside and plans to castle that way too, although on some occasions his king may even feel safer in the centre. Despite White's early action, Black's structure is still very sound. If Black can negotiate White's pressure or swap off into an ending then his chances of success are greater. For example, White's isolated pawn on h4 may then become more of a burden rather than an attacking unit.

Theoretical?

Not particularly so. Diagram 3 can veer off into many different variations, but the systems of development are more important than any particular sequence of moves.

Statistics

The Keres Attack is very popular, especially at higher levels, and its success rate is no secret. In *Mega Database 2002* I found more than 3,000 games with 6 g4, with White scoring an impressive 60%. It's mainly due to the strength of the Keres Attack that many players with Black now prefer using the Najdorf move order (with 5...a6), avoiding the Keres Attack entirely. Then Black can transpose into Scheveningen after, say, 6 Be2 e6 or 6 Be3 e6. Indeed, this has generally been Garry Kasparov's preferred move order.

Illustrative Games

Game 18
☐ **Anand** ■ **Ye Jiangchuan**
Kuala Lumpur 1989

1 e4 c5 2 Nf3 e6

In the introduction to the Scheveningen you will have noticed that Black played 2...d6 and 5...e6, but these moves are interchangeable.

3 d4 cxd4 4 Nxd4 Nf6 5 Nc3 d6 6 g4 h6 7 Rg1 Nc6 8 h4 h5 9 gxh5 Nxh5 10 Bg5 Nf6 11 Be2

White develops another piece and supports the possible advance h4-h5. White could also prepare queenside castling with 11 Qd2.

11...a6

Black more often than not plays this move in the Scheveningen. Two of its more obvious attributes are that it prevents a white piece coming to b5 and it prepares an eventual ...b7-b5.

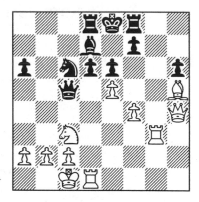

NOTE: ...a7-a6 is a typical Sicilian move.

12 h5 Bd7 13 Qd2 Be7

Another idea here is to begin queenside counterplay with 13...b5.

14 0-0-0 Qc7?

Black prepares to castle queenside. Outwardly, there seems nothing wrong with this move, but it allows a powerful white sequence.

14...b5, with a roughly level position, would have been stronger.

15 h6!

This move completely justifies White's previous play.

15...gxh6 16 Bxf6! Bxf6 (Diagram 4)

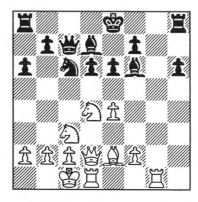

Diagram 4
White finds a spectacular move

Diagram 5
Black has to prevent Ne4

17 Nf5!!

If Black captures with the e6-pawn, then this leaves the d5-square vulnerable to attack and Black especially has to watch out for the c3-knight hopping into this square.

NOTE: Knight sacrifices on the f5-square are not uncommon in the Sicilian.

17...Be7

17...exf5 is met by the brilliant 18 Nd5 Qd8 19 Qxh6!! and Black is lost (19...Rxh6 allows 20 Rg8 mate).

18 Nxe7 Kxe7?

18...Nxe7 is more resilient, although White is clearly on the offensive.

19 Rg3!

In some cases the rook can swing over to d3 and attack the vulnerable d6-pawn.

19...b5 20 Qf4 Rad8 21 Qh4+ Ke8 22 Bxb5!

Another typical Sicilian sacrifice. Now 22...axb5 loses after 23 Nxb5 Qa5 24 Nxd6+ Kf8 25 Qf6 Rh7 26 Rdg1 Ne7 27 Rg7!.

WARNING: Beware of Bxb5 sacrifices in the Sicilian.

22...Ne5 23 Be2 Qc5 24 Bh5 Rf8

Of course, 24...Qxf2 loses to 25 Rg8+.

25 f4 Nc6 26 e5! (Diagram 5)

Threatening Ne4.

26...d5 27 Bxf7+!

The final combination.

27...Rxf7

Or 27...Kxf7 28 Qh5+ Ke7 29 Rg7+ and White mates.

28 Rg8+ Qf8

Black is forced to give up his queen. 28...Rf8 29 Qh5+ Ke7 30 Rg7+ again mates for White.

29 Rxf8+ Rxf8 30 Qh5+ Ke7 31 Qxh6 Black resigns

Game 19
□ Movsesian ■ Cvitan
German Bundesliga 1997

---

1 e4 c5 2 Nf3 e6 3 d4 cxd4 4 Nxd4 Nf6 5 Nc3 d6 6 g4 Nc6

On this occasion Black ignores White's space-gaining operation on the kingside and gets on with development.

7 g5

Naturally, White carries out his plan.

7...Nd7

The most natural retreat square for the knight.

8 Bc3

White continues to develop and plans queenside castling.

8...Be7 9 h4

Defending the g5-pawn and gaining space on the kingside.

9...0-0 (Diagram 6)

Black has made normal developing moves and has castled, but looking at the diagram position it's difficult to describe his king as safe. It's more as if it's castled into a storm!

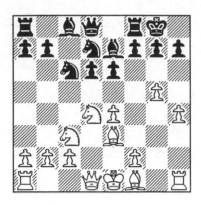

Diagram 6
'Castling into it'

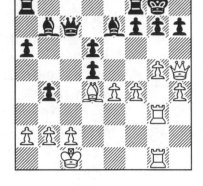

Diagram 7
Can you spot the idea?

10 Qh5!

White's queen moves menacingly towards the black king. Black's position is just about playable but not many players have the required nerves of steel.

10...a6 11 0-0-0 Nxd4 12 Bxd4 b5 13 Bd3

White can also continue his attack with 13 f4 or 13 e5!?.

13...Ne5 14 f4 Nxd3+ 15 Rxd3 Bb7 16 Rg1!

This is stronger than defending the e4-pawn with 16 Re1. White plans to open up the g-file. But how?

16...b4 17 Nd5!

In Game 18 we saw a typical Nf5 sacrifice. Here we see a customary Nd5 sacrifice. White buys time for his attack by blocking out the b7-bishop for a crucial move. After the limp 17 Ne2? Bxe4 Black suddenly possesses a monster bishop, both in defence and attack.

17...exd5?

An easy mistake to make, but 17...Bxd5 is more resilient. White's attack now seems to win.

18 Rdg3!

Crude but effective. In some lines White simply plans to blast open with g5-g6. For example: 18...Re8 19 g6! fxg6 20 Rxg6 hxg6 21 Qxg6 and White wins after 21...Bf8 22 Bxg7 Qd7 23 Bf6+ Bg7 24 Bxg7 etc.

18...Qc7 (Diagram 7) 19 Qh6!!

This is White's other big 'hit'. Now Black must sacrifice back more material to avoid mate.

19...Qxc2+!

This counter-sacrifice is in fact the only move to avoid immediate defeat: 19...gxh6 20 gxh6+ and it's mate next move; or 19...f6 and 20 gxf6 is a killer.

20 Kxc2 Rfc8+ 21 Kd2 gxh6 22 gxh6+ Bg5

22...Kf8 allows 23 Rg8 mate so Black is forced to give up the bishop.

23 Rxg5+ Kf8 24 exd5 Ke7 25 Rf5

As a contest, it's all over. White is a pawn up and his attack is still as menacing as ever.

25...Rc4 26 Kd3 Rac8 27 Rg7 Black resigns

The English Attack

1 e4 c5 2 Nf3 d6 3 d4 cxd4 4 Nxd4 Nf6 5 Nc3 e6 6 Be3 (Diagram 8)

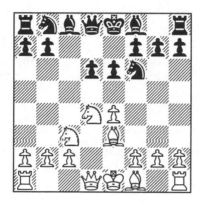

Diagram 8	Diagram 9
White plays 6 Be3	A typical position in the English Attack

We've already seen this move against the Najdorf and here White is aiming for pretty much the same sort of stuff: quick development of the queenside, queenside castling and a pawn storm on the kingside.

6...a6

This is Black's most popular response. He immediately sets queenside operations in motion. Classical development with 6...Nc6 is discussed in Game 21.

7 Qd2 b5 8 f3

Giving the e-pawn extra support and preparing g2-g4.

8...Nbd7

Black continues to develop on the queenside.

9 g4 h6

As against the Keres Attack, Black slows down White's play on the kingside with this move. The main alternative for Black is 9...Nb6, vacating the d7-square for the other knight in anticipation of g4-g5.

10 0-0-0 Bb7 (Diagram 9)

Strategies

It's safe to say that White will once again be concentrating his energies into a kingside offensive. White will want to dislodge the black knight on f6 with g4-g5, and this move will usually require some preparation. Black will often hit back with ...b5-b4, followed by the typical freeing advance ...d7-d5. Black's king may often simply remain in the centre as it's normally safer there than it would be on the kingside. Play is extremely sharp and one slight error can often be enough for a decisive advantage.

Theoretical?

A large body of theory has built up over the last twenty years and it's advisable, especially for anyone playing Black, to read up before attempting to play this line in a serious game. That said, the theoretical moves are usually the most logical ones, so playing on general principles can be sufficient in many cases (unlike, say, in the Yugoslav Attack against the Dragon).

Statistics

6 Be3 is now one of the most popular responses to the Scheveningen. One of its appeals is that white players can adopt the same system against both the Najdorf and the Scheveningen, thus cutting down on the number of systems to learn.

Looking at the positions further down the line, I found just under 500 games from Diagram 9 in *Mega Database 2002*. White scores a reasonable 55%, while as many as 75% of the games are decisive.

Illustrative Games

Game 20
□ **Mastrovasilis** ■ **Lutz**
Corfu 1999

1 e4 c5 2 Nf3 d6 3 d4 cxd4 4 Nxd4 Nf6 5 Nc3 a6

The game starts off as a Najdorf, but soon transposes into a Scheveningen.

6 f3 e6 7 Be3 b5 8 g4

In the introduction to the English Attack White was delaying this move in favour of 8 Qd2, but these moves are often interchangeable.

8...h6 9 Qd2 Nbd7 10 0-0-0 Bb7 11 h4

A typical move. White gets ready to prepare the g4-g5 lunge.

11...b4 12 Nb1

12 Na4 and 12 Nce2 are also very playable moves and both have built up a vast mountain of theory.

12...d5

Now that the knight on c3 has been displaced, Black is in a good position to play this freeing ...d6-d5 advance. With White's pawns flying down the kingside, Black is in no hurry to castle. If anything, his king is safest in the centre!

NOTE: The move ...d6-d5 is a crucial freeing advance in many lines of the Sicilian.

13 Bh3

Now White threatens g4-g5.

13...g5!

Typically uncompromising play. Black sacrifices a pawn in order to delay White's advance on the kingside. I believe it was the Bulgarian Grandmaster Veselin Topalov who first came up with this idea.

14 hxg5 hxg5 15 exd5 Nxd5 16 Bxg5 Qb6 17 Bg2 Rxh1 18 Bxh1

White is a pawn up but his attack has been slowed down a little. This gives Black the chance to commence serious counterplay on the queenside.

18...Rc8 19 Re1 Nc5 20 f4 Bg7 21 Nf5 Kf8 22 Nxg7 (Diagram 10)

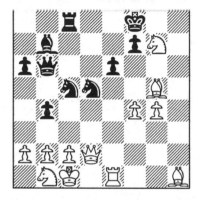

Diagram 10
Black recaptures on g7, right?

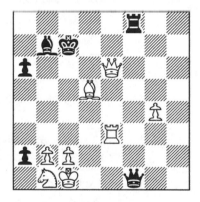

Diagram 11
Black has the last laugh

22...b3!!

An amazing move. Black simply ignore the knight on g7 and goes ahead with his attack. In some lines the idea is simply to promote to a new queen with ...bxa2 and ...a2-a1Q.

23 Qd4 Nd3+!

Black gives up another piece to keep his attack running. 23...bxa2 24 Nxe6+ fxe6 (not 24...Nxe6 25 Qh8 mate) 25 Qh8+ Kf7 26 Qh7+ Kf8 leads to a draw by perpetual check.

24 Qxd3 Qf2 25 Nxe6+

Or 25 Re2 Qf1+ 26 Qd1 Qxd1+ 27 Kxd1 bxa2+ and the pawn queens.

25...fxe6?

As far as I can see, White doesn't seem to have a good continuation after the calm 25...Kg8!. There is no good defence to all of Black's threats.

26 Bh6+ Ke7 27 Qh7+?

Now it's White's turn to err, although this is hardly surprising in such a complex position. White should play 27 Bg5+! Kd6 28 Rxe6+ Kxe6 29 Bxd5+ Bxd5 30 Qf5+ Kd6 31 Qe5+ Kc6 32 cxb3, after which the position remains very unclear.

27...Kd6!

Black's king looks as in as much danger as White's, but Lutz has it all worked out.

28 Bf8+

Now 28 Rxe6+ doesn't work so well: 28...Kxe6 29 Bxd5+ Bxd5 30 Qf5+ Kd6 31 Qe5+ Kc6 32 cxb3 Qg1+ 33 Kc2 Qh2+ and the bishop hangs on h6.

28...Rxf8 29 Qe4 bxa2 30 Qxe6+ Kc7 31 Bxd5 Qxf4+ 32 Re3

Or 32 Kd1 axb1Q+ 33 Ke2 Qxc2 mate.

32...Qf1+ (Diagram 11)

This check is decisive.

33 Re1

Exercise 3: How does Black meet 33 Kd2 here?

33...Qf4+ 34 Re3 Bxd5 35 Qe7+ Kb8 White resigns

Game 21
□ **Fischer** ■ **Spassky**
Belgrade (25th matchgame) 1992

---

1 e4 c5 2 Nc3 Nc6 3 Nge2

Once again we see White employing an unusual move order, but soon an Open Sicilian position is reached.

3...d6 4 d4 cxd4 5 Nxd4 e6 6 Be3 Nf6 7 Qd2 Be7 8 f3 a6 9 0-0-0 0-0 10 g4

In this game Black has developed classically and has castled before thinking about queenside operations. Black wants to play ...b7-b5, so he exchanges knights first.

10...Nxd4 11 Bxd4 b5 12 g5 Nd7

The knight moves to its normal retreat square.

NOTE: The d7-square is the most natural retreat for the f6-knight.

13 h4 b4

Now White must choose where to put this knight – not an easy task.

14 Na4!?

On a4 the knight can be useful as a blocker of the black attack. On the other hand, the knight could also become vulnerable to attack itself. White's two other choices were 14 Ne2 and 14 Nb1.

14...Bb7?!

This allows White to perform a clever combination. After 14...Qa5 the position would be roughly level, with both sides having good opportunities to attack.

15 Nb6!

A nice trick to exchange off the knights. Black was hoping for 15 Qxb4?! Bc6, which gives Black good compensation for the pawn in the form of open lines to attack the white king.

15...Rb8

15...Nxb6 16 Qxb4 skewers the minor pieces and wins one back.

16 Nxd7 Qxd7 17 Kb1 Qc7 18 Bd3

White is slightly ahead in the attacking race and this advantage becomes more pronounced after Black's next move.

18...Bc8?

Black plans ...e6-e5 and ...Be6, but this is too slow.

19 h5 e5 20 Be3 Be6 21 Rdg1 (Diagram 12)

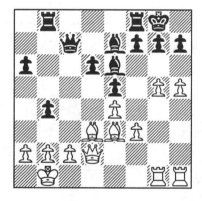
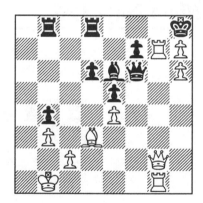

Diagram 12	**Diagram 13**
White is in command	White dominates the g-file!

It's now quite obvious by looking at the position that White is much further ahead than Black in the attacking race.

21...a5 22 g6!

Crucially, the right way to proceed. The careless 22 h6? would undo all of White's previous good work and allow Black to block the attack with the simple 22...g6. White's offensive would then be at a dead end.

TIP: Choosing the correct pawn break is a crucial element of carrying out an effective attack.

22...Bf6

Trying to block with 22...h6 is no use: 23 Bxh6! gxh6 24 Qxh6 gives White a mating attack.

23 gxh7+ Kh8!

This is often seen as a defensive procedure. Instead of capturing the pawn, Black uses it as a defensive wall against its own pieces.

24 Bg5!

This defensive bishop is holding Black's position together, so White naturally wishes to trade it off.

24...Qe7 25 Rg3

Preparing to double on the g-file.

25...Bxg5 26 Rxg5 Qf6 27 Rhg1 Qxf3 28 Rxg7 Qf6?

28...Qf4 is Black's last chance to stay in the game.

29 h6 a4 30 b3 axb3 31 axb3 Rfd8 32 Qg2! (Diagram 13)

The tripling on the g-file is decisive. Black has no defence to the threats.

32...Rf8 33 Rg8+! Kxh7 34 Rg7+ Kh8 35 h7 Black resigns

Black has no good defence to the threat of 36 Rg8+ Kxh7 37 Qh2+ Qh6 38 R1g7 mate.

White Plays Be2

1 e4 c5 2 Nf3 d6 3 d4 cxd4 4 Nxd4 Nf6 5 Nc3 e6 6 Be2 (Diagram 14)

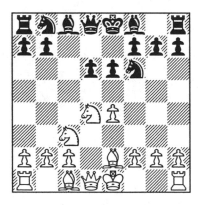

Diagram 14
White plays 6 Be2

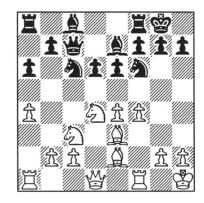

Diagram 15
A typical Classical Scheveningen

The classical approach. With this move, White plans to develop his pieces and castle kingside before undertaking any active operations.

6...a6

The most popular choice, although Black can also play without this move for the time being, simply continuing with ...Be7, ...0-0 and ...Nc6.

7 0-0 Be7 8 f4

A typical move in the Classical Scheveningen. White gains space on the kingside and some control over the e5-square.

8...0-0

Once again Black could consider delaying castling, but the immediate lunge 8...b5 looks a bit premature. For example: 9 Bf3 Bb7 10 e5! forces 10...Nd5 and 11 Nxd5 Bxd5 12 Bxd5 exd5 13 e6 looks nice for White.

9 Be3 Nc6

9...Qc7, delaying the development of the knight, is also possible, although this very often simply transposes into the main line after 10 a4 Nc6.

10 a4

It's noticeable that White is generally playing in a more restrained manner than in the Keres or the English Attack. White wants an eventual attack, but a much more controlled one where Black's counterplay is at a minimum.

For the more direct 10 Qe1, see Game 23.

10...Qc7 11 Kh1 (Diagram 15)

Once again we see this little king move, played in order to negate various tactics along the g1-a7 diagonal.

Strategies

White is planning on a slow-burning attack on the kingside. There are a few possible ways to carry out the attack, but the most popular procedure involves the plan of g4-g5, once again displacing the crucial defensive knight from f6. White often plays Bf3-g2, clearing the way for the white queen to enter the attack, perhaps via h5, while giving the king on h1 some much needed added protection. Sometimes White's rook on f1 makes a journey to h3 via f3. This, coupled with the queen on h5, already produces very dangerous threats against the black king.

Black has to consider how to both fortify his king's position and accomplish counterplay in the centre and on the queenside. The first objective is often achieved by some deep and prophylactic defensive measures. For example, Black can move the rook to e8, play ...Bf8, ...g7-g6, ...Bg7 and finally ...Nf6-d7-f8, protecting the crucial h7-pawn. This procedure is quite lengthy but produces an extremely resilient defensive position. More aggressively, Black may play ...b7-b6 followed by ...Bc8-b7, pointing this bishop along the long diagonal directly opposite White's king. Black will also be on the lookout for any chance to play a freeing ...d6-d5 or ...e6-e5 advance.

Theoretical?

Not particularly so. In this position plans are more important than any particular moves.

Statistics

6 Be2 is still the most popular choice against the Scheveningen. It appeals to players as White seems to keep more control over the proceedings than with, say, the English Attack. It's less likely that a small error played by either side will be so crucial, as the attacking and defensive plans are longer and more deliberate. The popularity of the Classical Scheveningen can be gauged by the fact that there were over 2,000 examples of Diagram 15 in *Mega Database 2002*. White scores 56%, while 64% of the games are decisive (this is considerably lower than the figure in the English Attack).

Illustrative Games

Game 22
☐ **Lobron** ■ **Van Wely**
Antwerp 1996

1 e4 c5 2 Nf3 d6 3 d4 cxd4 4 Nxd4 Nf6 5 Nc3 a6 6 Be2 e6 7 0-0 Be7 8 f4 0-0 9 Kh1 Qc7 10 a4 Nc6 11 Be3

Reaching the 'normal' position.

11...Re8!

Black begins his defensive preparations on the kingside.

12 Bf3

A good prophylactic measure against Black's queenside counterplay.

12...Bd7

Black would like to fianchetto this bishop, but 12...b6 13 Nxc6 Qxc6 14 e5 wins material for White. Instead Black intends to exchange on d4 and put the bishop on c6.

13 Nb3!

White puts a stop to Black's plan by avoiding exchanges. 13 g4 Nxd4! 14 Bxd4 Bc6 15 g5 Nd7 gives Black an ideal defensive set-up.

TIP: In general, the side with less space should seek exchanges, while the side with more space should avoid them.

13...b6 14 g4! (Diagram 16)

The logical follow-up. White intends g4-g5.

14...Bc8!

At first it's extremely difficult to get to grips with such a move. After all, didn't this bishop just move from c8 to d7 just a couple of moves ago? And now it's moving back! How can Black justify such an apparent loss of time?

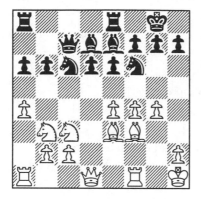

Diagram 16
The threat is g4-g5

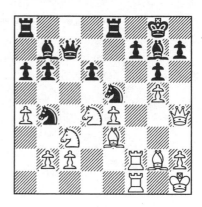

Diagram 17
Black has a good defensive set-up.

Well, the overriding factor here is that the f6-knight needs a good square to retreat to after g4-g5. At the moment it has none, but after the bishop moves it can go to its natural retreat square of d7. From here it can always go back to f8, where it protects the crucial h7-square (see later on as to why this is so important). About the loss of 'two tempi' with ...Bc8-d7-c8, well Black can always point to the fact that White has spent one of these moves just retreating his knight from the apparently aggressive d4-square to the obviously more passive b3-square.

In the Keres and the English Attacks Black often forestalls White's advance with ...h7-h6. Here, with his king already committed to the kingside, this makes no sense. After 14...h6?! White will follow up with 15 h4 and the opening of the kingside after g4-g5 can only favour White.

15 g5 Nd7 16 Bg2!

Clearing the way for the white queen to go to h5.

16...Bb7 17 Qh5 Nb4

Releasing the power of the bishop along the diagonal and attacking the slightly vulnerable c2-pawn.

An example of how careful Black has to be in these positions can be seen in an earlier game involving the same player with the black pieces, which continued 17...g6 18 Qh3 Nb4? 19 f5! Nxc2? 20 fxg6 fxg6 21 Rf7!! and Black was in big trouble because 21...Kxf7 22 Qxh7+ Kf8 23 Rf1+ is the end (Tiviakov-Van Wely, Groningen 1995).

18 Nd4

White correctly takes time out to defend c2. The blunt 18 Rf3? is ineffective here. After 18...Nxc2 19 Rh3 Nf8 Black more than adequately defends the h7-square (an advantage of having the knight on d7).

18...g6 19 Qh4 e5!

Black strikes back in the centre. Now Black obtains a typical outpost on e5 for the knight.

20 fxe5 Nxe5 21 Rf2 Bf8!

Manoeuvring the bishop to g7.

22 Raf1 Bg7 (Diagram 17)

Black can be well satisfied with his work. The bishop on g7 and the knight on e5 are very useful defensive pieces.

23 Nf3 Re7 24 Nxe5 Bxe5 25 Bf4 Rf8 26 Bxe5 Rxe5 27 Qh6 Qe7 28 Rf6 Bxe4!

The counter-attack begins!

29 Nxe4 Rxe4 30 Bxe4?

A mistake. Van Wely gives 30 c3! Nd3 31 Bxe4 Qxe4+ 32 Kg1 Qe3+ and Black draws by perpetual check.

30...Qxe4+ 31 Kg1 Nd5 32 Qh3

Or 32 R6f2 Ne3 33 Re1 Qg4+ 34 Kh1 Nf5 and White is forced to give up the exchange.

32...Nxf6 33 gxf6 h5

Black is a pawn up and it's White's king who is the most vulnerable.

34 Qg3 Qxc2 35 Qxd6 Qxb2 36 Rd1 Re8 37 Qe7 Rc8 38 Qd7 Qc3 39 Rd6 White resigns

Black delivers mate after 39...Qe1+ 40 Kg2 Rc2+ 41 Kf3 Rf2+ 42 Kg3 Qe3+ 43 Kh4 Rf4+ 44 Kg5 Rg4.

Game 23
□ **Shirov** ■ **Benjamin**
Horgen 1994

---

1 e4 c5 2 Nf3 e6 3 d4 cxd4 4 Nxd4 Nc6 5 Nc3 a6 6 Be2 Qc7 7 Be3 Nf6 8 0-0 Be7 9 f4 d6

What began as a Taimanov Sicilian (see Chapter 6) has now transposed into the Classical Scheveningen.

10 Qe1

This is more direct than 10 a4. White doesn't bother to take steps to prevent ...b7-b5.

10...0-0 11 Qg3 Nxd4

The immediate 11...b5 is premature: 12 e5! dxe5 13 Nxc6 Qxc6 14 fxe5 Ne4 (otherwise Bf3 is coming) 15 Nxe4 Qxe4 16 Bd3 Qh4 (16...Qc6 17 Bh6!) 17 Qxh4 Bxh4 18 Be4 Rb8 19 Ba7 and White wins material. 11...Bd7 is possible, though.

12 Bxd4 b5 13 a3

Preventing ...b5-b4.

13...Bb7 14 Kh1 Bc6!?

Preparing ...Qb7 and perhaps ...b5-b4.

15 Rae1

White slowly builds on the kingside.

15...Qb7 16 Bd3 (Diagram 18)

The immediate lunge with 16 e5 is not worrisome for Black. After 16...dxe5 17 fxe5 Ne4 18 Nxe4 Bxe4 the bishop does a good job on e4.

16...b4

16...a5 looks like a useful preparatory move, but 17 e5 has more punch now that the e4-square is not available to Black: 17...dxe5 18 fxe5 Nd7 19 Ne4 and White's initiative is beginning to look threatening.

17 Nd1!

The knight plans to join the action on the kingside.

17...g6 18 Nf2 bxa3 19 bxa3 Nh5 20 Qe3! Nxf4?!

As an improvement, Shirov suggests striking back with 20...f5!?.

21 Qxf4 e5

Black wins the piece back with a fork, but Shirov has a surprise in store.

22 Ng4!

Now 22...exf4 allows 23 Nh6 mate!

22...f6?

Black should enter the complications of 22...exd4 23 Nh6+ Kg7 24 Nxf7.

23 Bc4+ Kh8 24 Nxe5! dxe5 (Diagram 19)

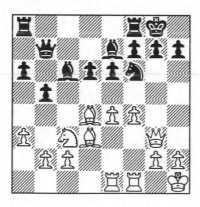

Diagram 18
White is lining up an attack

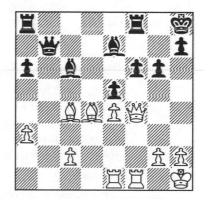

Diagram 19
Can you see a flashy move?

25 Qxe5!

Very flash, although 25 Bxe5 looks just as strong.

25...Kg7

Taking the queen is no good: 25...fxe5 26 Bxe5+ Rf6 (or 26...Bf6 27 Rxf6 Kg7 28 Rf7+ Kh6 29 Bg7+ Kg5 30 Rxb7 Bxb7 31 Bxf8 Rxf8 32 Bd3 and White is two pawns up) 27 Rxf6 Kg7 28 Rxc6+, followed by Bd5 – Shirov.

26 Qf4

Now White remains a pawn up and still has the attack.

26...Rad8 27 c3 h6 28 Rb1 Qa8 29 Rb6 Rxd4 30 cxd4 Bxe4 31 Re1 f5?! 32 Qe5+ Bf6 33 Rxf6 Black resigns

33...Rxf6 loses to 34 Qe7+.

The Fischer Attack

1 e4 c5 2 Nf3 d6 3 d4 cxd4 4 Nxd4 Nf6 5 Nc3 e6 6 Bc4 (Diagram 20)

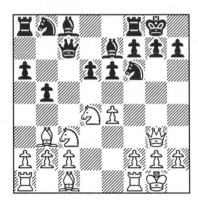

Diagram 20
White plays 6 Bc4

Diagram 21
A typical Fischer Attack position

6 Bc4 is a huge favourite of Bobby Fischer's and has also been played by the likes of Garry Kasparov and Nigel Short (against Garry Kasparov!). The king's bishop is aggressively placed on c4, although it has to be said that at the moment the pawn on e6 does a very good job of blunting its power. However, on the a2-g8 diagonal the bishop dissuades Black from playing either ...d6-d5 or ...e6-e5, both of which would certainly bring the bishop to life.

6...a6

It should be noted that this position often arises out of the Najdorf move order 5...a6 6 Bc4 e6. Another possibility for Black is 6...Nc6, which is dealt with in the Classical Sicilian (see Chapter 5).

7 Bb3

A prophylactic measure against both ...d6-d5 and the impending ...b7-b5.

7...b5

Black seeks immediate counterplay on the queenside. Also possible are the developing 7...Be7 and 7...Nbd7, planning ...Nc5 which will attack the bishop and put extra pressure on the e4-pawn.

8 0-0 Be7 9 Qf3

This is very much the modern way for White to play, attacking first with pieces rather than looking for a particular pawn break. The more traditional approach is with 9 f4, planning f4-f5, to put pressure on the e6-pawn and try to bring the bishop on b3 to life. Play can continue 9...Bb7 10 f5 e5 11 Nde2 and now 11...Nxe4 12 Nxe4 Bxe4 13 Nc3 Bb7 14 Qg4 gives White excellent compensation for the pawn, so Black should probably be content with 11...Nbd7.

9...Qc7

Black must display caution here as White's last move contained a threat. For example: 9...0-0? 10 e5! wins material. The most natural move way to deal with this threat is with 9...Bb7, but this allows White to carry out a very effective sacrifice: 10 Bxe6! fxe6 11 Nxe6 Qd7 12 Nxg7+ Kf7 13 Nf5 and White has three very good pawns for the piece, while Black's king is in disarray.

TIP: Bxe6 is a trick to look out for in the Fischer Attack.

Black's only other sensible move at this point is 9...Qb6. Both this and 9...Qc7 plan to meet 10 e5? with 10...Bb7!.

10 Qg3

White turns his attentions to Black's g-pawn.

10...0-0 (Diagram 21)

Black is not forced to protect g7. Another major possibility here is 10...Nc6 11 Nxc6 Qxc6. Now White can grab on g7, but after 12 Qxg7 Rg8 13 Qh6 Nxe4 14 Nxe4 Qxe4 the capture of the crucial e4-pawn is more important and Black stands well. Instead, White normally opts to defend e4 with 12 Re1.

Strategies

From Diagram 21 White has two main approaches, which can often be combined. The first is simply to attack the kingside with pieces. This will generally not work against a very solid structure, but here White has more chances as his pieces are extremely actively placed. This plan can be supplemented by the positional thrust f2-f4-f5, adding pressure on the e6-pawn. After either a capture on f5 or a the advance to ...e6-e5, White's bishop comes to life on b3.

For his part, Black has no weaknesses in his position and if he extinguishes White's early initiative then he has good chances to exploit his better pawn structure. Black will probably have quite a bit of defending to do, at least to start with, but counterplay can be found on the queenside and against White's slightly vulnerable e4-pawn.

Theoretical?

It's especially important for black players to read up on this line as this system is quite unforgiving: one slip and Black could be facing an overwhelming attack. However, theory does state that Black is doing okay (if he knows what he's doing!).

Statistics

Taking the position after 6...a6 (to include the more common Najdorf move order), this position has been reached over 7,000 times in *Mega Database 2002*. White scores a below-par 50% and 74% of the games are decisive.

Illustrative Game

Game 24
□ **Kasparov** ■ **Gelfand**
Linares 1993

1 e4 c5 2 Nf3 d6 3 d4 cxd4 4 Nxd4 Nf6 5 Nc3 a6 6 Bc4 e6 7 Bb3 b5 8 0-0 Be7 9 Qf3 Qc7 10 Qg3 0-0 11 Bh6!

Forcing the knight on f6 to retreat, as 11...Nh5?! 12 Qg4! is annoying for Black.

11...Ne8 12 Rad1 Bd7 13 Nf3!?

White plays very much with his pieces and begins to point them in the direction of the black king. A different plan would begin with 13 f4, intending f4-f5.

13...b4?!

This is a bit too provocative, especially against someone of Kasparov's attacking prowess. Black should really start thinking about completing development; 13...Nc6! is much stronger.

14 Ne2!

Another piece goes to the kingside.

14...a5 (Diagram 22)

Threatening to trap the bishop with ...a5-a4, but Black is doing nothing about defence!

15 Nf4! Kh8

15...a4? loses after 16 Bxg7! Nxg7 17 Nh5 Bf6 18 Nxf6+ Kh8 19 Qh4 h5 20 Qf4 and it will be mate with Qh6.

16 Bg5 Nf6 17 Qh4! Bb5?

The final mistake. Black has to try 17...Nc6.

18 Nd4! Be8

Or 18...Bxf1 19 Ndxe6! fxe6 20 Bxe6 (threatening Ng6 mate) 20...g6 (20...h6 21 Bxh6) 21 Nxg6+ Kg7 22 Qh6 mate.

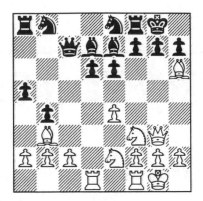

Diagram 22
Black neglects his defensive duties

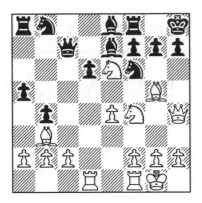

Diagram 23
White to play and win

19 Ndxe6! (Diagram 23)

This sacrifice is killing.

19...fxe6 20 Nxe6 Qa7 21 e5! dxe5 22 Nxf8 Bxf8 23 Bxf6 gxf6 24 Rd8 Nd7 25 Qg4! Black resigns

After 25...Bg7 26 Qe6! White mates with Qg8.

Summary

1) With its solid pawn structure and no weaknesses, the Scheveningen is an ideal choice for those wishing to play from a sound positional basis.

2) The Keres Attack with 6 g4 is without doubt the most dangerous white system against the Scheveningen and scores well in practice. This has led to many black players to transpose into the Scheveningen via the Najdorf move-order, which avoids the Keres Attack.

3) The English Attack with f2-f3, Be3 and Qd2 is becoming more and more popular and is a relatively straightforward line for White to play. The bonus for white players is that they can adopt the same attacking set-up against both the Najdorf and the Scheveningen, thus reducing the amount of learning time.

4) If White is looking for a more controlled attacking game then the 6 Be2 variation is an ideal choice.

Chapter Four

The Sveshnikov Variation

1 e4 c5 2 Nf3 Nc6 3 d4 cxd4 4 Nxd4 Nf6 5 Nc3 e5 (Diagram 1)

Diagram 1
Black plays 5...e5

The Sveshnikov Variation is a modern, aggressive and uncompromising way to play the Sicilian. On move five Black immediately strikes in the centre with his e-pawn, attacking the white knight on d4 and forcing it to move from its central post. Emanuel Lasker first brought this move to prominence when he tried it in his 1910 World Championship match with Carl Schlechter. The defence didn't really catch on, even after the Argentinean IM Jorge Pelikan injected some new ideas for Black in the 1950s. The opening only really began to achieve widespread popularity in the 1970s, when the young Russian player Evgeny Sveshnikov refined the system and used it with great success. Players of all standards began to appreciate its potential and now there is hardly a major international tournament without a Sveshnikov battle or two.

A word or two about the name. In its time the variation has been referred to as the Pelikan or even the Lasker-Pelikan, but most players now refer to it as the Sveshnikov (at least the variation beginning with 8...b5).

The Opening Moves

The following sequence of moves has been repeated thousands of times in club and tournament chess. It is worth a little time and space, however, to explain just what each side is trying to do.

1 e4 c5 2 Nf3 Nc6

So far we've concentrated on 2...d6, but 2...Nc6 is a popular move which can introduce quite a few Sicilian variations, for example: the Classical (see Chapter 5), the Taimanov and the Accelerated Dragon (Chapter 6).

3 d4 cxd4 4 Nxd4 Nf6 5 Nc3 e5

Immediately White must make a decision with his knight.

6 Ndb5!

So-called 'normal' Sicilian rules do not quite apply here. In the Najdorf Variation we are used to seeing the knight retreating to b3, or possibly f3, but here the white knight ventures to b5. There are two reasons for this. Firstly, the one major negative effect of Black's previous move is that the d5- and d6-squares are now permanently weakened and are thus difficult for Black to defend. By playing Nbd5, White immediately homes in on the weakness of the d6-square. For example, the move 6...a6?! is simply answered by 7 Nd6+ Bxd6 (who would want to play 7...Ke7 here?) 8 Qxd6 and Black really misses his dark-squared bishop.

The other reason for 6 Ndb5 is that simply no other move challenges Black's basic strategy. For example: 6 Nb3?! Bb4! and Black has it all: he is ahead on development, threatens the e4-pawn and will follow up with the freeing ...d7-d5. The only other vaguely challenging move looks to be 6 Nf5, but Black has a good and direct answer to this: 6...d5!, uncovering an attack on the f5. After 7 exd5 Bxf5 8 dxc6 bxc6 Black is very comfortably placed.

It should be said that 6 Nxc6? would be an instructive error on White's part. After 6...bxc6 Black strengthens his centre (especially the d5-square) and prepares to play the ...d7-d5 advance.

WARNING: White should have a good reason for exchanging knights on c6, especially if Black can strengthen his centre by recapturing with the b-pawn.

6...d6

A necessity. Black must prevent the white knight from entering the d6-square. Now White has succeeded in preventing Black from playing an early ...d7-d5 and the bishop on f8 is hemmed in behind the d6-pawn. On the negative side, the knight on b5 will soon be forced back to a miserable square on the side of the board.

7 Bg5

A very logical move, pinning the f6-knight to the black queen. White will soon be able to inflict more weaknesses in the black camp.

A totally different way of playing the position is with 7 Nd5!?. Due to the threat of Nc7+, Black is forced to play 7...Nxd5 and after 8 exd5 a position untypical of the 'normal' Sveshnikov is reached. One advantage for Black over the usual lines is that the 'hole' on d5 has been filled by a white pawn and this square is no longer a weakness in the black camp. One possible variation is 8...Nb8 9 c4 a6 10 Nc3 Be7 11 Be2 0-0 12 0-0 f5, after which White will try to utilise his pawn majority on the queenside. In contrast, Black will look for counterplay on the kingside, where he has the extra pawn.

7...a6

Pushing the annoying knight away. 7...Be7? is a mistake: following 8 Bxf6 Black must still capture with the g-pawn as 8...Bxf6 allows 9 Nxd6+.

8 Na3

8 Bxf6 is also possible, after which Black must capture with the g-pawn (8...Qxf6?? allows 9 Nc7+). Now 8...gxf6 9 Na3 b5 transposes into the main line (although Black can also consider playing 9...f5).

8...b5!

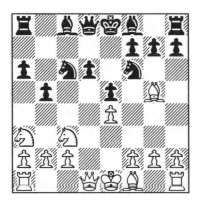

Diagram 2
The starting position for the Sveshnikov

In the early days of this line, black players were opting for the developing move 8...Be6, but the text move is much more to the point. Crucially, Black's lunge on the queenside prevents White's knight on a3 from re-entering the game via c4. A by-product of 8...b5! is that Black also threatens a simple pawn fork with ...b5-b4.

This is the main starting position of the Sveshnikov. Structurally, Black's position is a little bit of a mess. White has total control of the d5-square and on White's next move he can inflict more weaknesses on Black with 9 Bxf6 gxf6 (9...Qxf6 10 Nd5 is good for White – see later). The one big price that White has to pay for all this structural advantage is that he currently possesses the worst placed piece on the board: that poor knight which has moved four times only to wind up on the miserable a3-square. White will inevitably have to spend time relocating this knight to greener pastures and Black can put this time to good use and develop the potential he has in his position.

There are two main lines for White from this position and we will look at them both in turn.

White plays 9 Bxf6

1 e4 c5 2 Nf3 Nc6 3 d4 cxd4 4 Nxd4 Nf6 5 Nc3 e5 6 Ndb5 d6 7 Bg5 a6 8 Na3 b5 9 Bxf6

The main line. White immediate inflicts another weakness in Black's position: doubled f-pawns.

9...gxf6

Recapturing with 9...Qxf6 avoids doubled pawns but loses too much time. After 10 Nd5 Qd8 11 c3 (11 c4 also looks promising) 11...Be7 12 Nc2 White is a tempo up over 9 Nd5 Be7 lines.

10 Nd5

Occupying the juicy d5-outpost and taking care of the ...b5-b4 threat.

10...f5

With this move Black starts his fightback for the control of the centre. Striking out with his doubled f-pawn, Black hits White's important e4-pawn, which at the moment guarantees White control of the crucial d5-square.

Another way for Black to play the position is with 10...Bg7, preparing ...Nc6-e7. But not the immediate 10...Ne7??, which allows an embarrassing mate in one with 11 Nxf6!

11 c3

A typical move in the Sveshnikov. White begins the slow relocation of his worst placed minor piece, which will want to re-enter the game via c2 and e3.

NOTE: The relocation of White's a3-knight is an integral part of the Sveshnikov.

You'll not be surprised to learn that White has other choices here. The most extreme of these is the speculative sacrifice 11 Bxb5!?, a direct attempt to blow Black's position apart. After 11...axb5 12 Nxb5 Ra4 13 Nbc7+ Kd7 there are massive complications, but Black seems to be holding his own, as long as he knows what he's doing. Another try for White is the developing move 11 Bd3, the subject of Game 26. Finally, there is 11 exf5, which can transpose to the text after 11...Bxf5 12 c3 Bg7 13 Nc2.

11...Bg7

11...fxe4? is too greedy. Now the sacrifice 12 Bxb5! axb5 13 Nxb5 is very powerful, as 13...Ra5? 14 Nbc7+ Kd7 15 Qg4+ leads to mate.

With 11...Bg7 Black is preparing to castle. Now a capture on e4 is threatened so White resolves the tension.

12 exf5 Bxf5 13 Nc2 0-0 14 Nce3

White has spent nearly half his moves on this one piece! Finally the knight rejoins the main action in the centre, gaining time by attacking the f5-bishop.

14...Be6

The strongest retreat for the bishop. From here it can keep an eye on both the d5- and the f5-squares.

15 Bd3

White finally develops the f1-bishop and prepares to castle. Another possible way forward is with 15 g3, intending to fianchetto with Bg2.

15...f5 (Diagram 3)

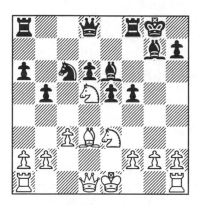

Diagram 3
Black plays ...f5 for the second time!

Strategies

Diagram 3 is a very sharp position in which both sides have chances to play for the initiative. Black's pawns on e5 and f5 very often hold the key to the position. If they can advance forward freely then Black can sometimes flood his pieces in behind them and produce a very strong attack against the white king. However, each advance has its negatives as well as its positives. If Black plays ...f5-f4, then this brings White's bishop on d3 to life. With a white queen on h5, Black would already be threatened with checkmate on h7. The other advance, ...e5-e4, blocks out White's light-squared bishop but presents White with the use of the f4-square for the d5-knight. It follows that Black must be very careful with these advances.

On White's part, he may attack Black's pawn structure with a timely a2-a4 or f2-f4. If White can exchange light-squared bishops Black sometimes has problems defending all of his weak squares. Black has more pawn weaknesses and these often become more important as the game goes on.

Theoretical?

Once the players reach Diagram 3, general principles along with a little theoretical knowledge should be sufficient. Black players, however, should be wary of earlier possibilities for White, including 11 Bd3 and the ultra-sharp 11 Bxb5!?.

Statistics

This is a very popular line, with over a third of all games with 5...e5 reaching the position after 9 Bxf6 gxf6. I found nearly 6,000 games in *Mega Database 2002*, with White scoring 54%. The complexity of the positions is reflected by the fact that 69% of the games lead to decisive results.

Illustrative Games

Game 25
□ **Topalov** ■ **Van Wely**
Wijk aan Zee 1999

1 e4 c5 2 Nf3 Nc6 3 d4 cxd4 4 Nxd4 Nf6 5 Nc3 e5 6 Ndb5 d6 7 Bg5 a6 8 Na3 b5 9 Bxf6 gxf6 10 Nd5 f5 11 c3 Bg7 12 exf5 Bxf5 13 Nc2 0-0 14 Nce3 Be6 15 Bd3 f5 16 0-0

White moves his king into safety. Another major option is the aggressive 16 Qh5!?.

16...e4!?

Immediately advancing in the centre. Black can also play preparatory moves such as 16...Ra7 (planning to swing across to the kingside) or 16...Kh8 (moving the king into relative safety).

17 Nf4

White reacts by utilising the newly attained outpost to attack the bishop on e6.

17...Bf7 18 Bc2 Be5 (Diagram 4)

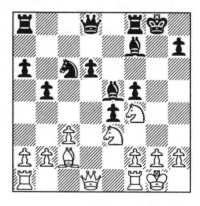
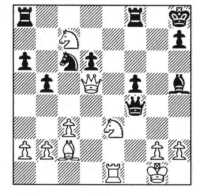

Diagram 4
Black begins kingside operations

Diagram 5
Black misses a great chance

Black points his dark-squared bishop at the white kingside.

19 Nfd5 Qg5 ˙

Now if White does nothing Black will push forward with ...f5-f4, so White strikes back on the kingside.

20 f4!

TIP: f2-f4 is often a useful move to break up Black's centre in the Sveshnikov.

20...exf3 21 Rxf3!?

After this move the game plunges into complications. Recapturing with the queen was also possible.

21...Bh5

Skewering the rook to the queen, apparently winning an exchange.

22 Nc7!

But White is also winning an exchange, as there is a dual threat of Nxa8 and Ne6.

22...Bf4 23 Qd5+ Kh8 24 Rxf4 Qxf4 25 Re1? (Diagram 5)

White makes the first error. In his notes, Van Wely gives 25 Qd2 Rae8 26 Nxe8 Rxe8 27 Re1. White is solidly placed and Black's weak pawns may become significant.

25...Rac8??

Van Wely misses a big chance to initiate a deadly attack: 25...Ne5! 26 Nxa8 Rg8!! (Black is temporarily a piece down but the attack is awesome) 27 g3 Rxg3+! 28 hxg3 Qxg3+ 29 Kf1 Qf4+ 30 Kg1 Nf3+ 31 Kf1 (or 31 Qxf3 Bxf3 32 Nc7 Qg3+ 33 Kf1 f4) 31...Nxe1+ 32 Kxe1 Qxe3+ 33 Kf1 Qe2+ 34 Kg1 Qxc2 and it's now Black who is up on material.

26 Ne6

Now White regains control.

26...Qh4 27 g3 Rg8 28 Nxf5

Black still has a rook for knight, but his position is collapsing. White's knights are real monsters!

28...Qc4 29 Qxd6 Rg6 30 Ne7 Nxe7 31 Qe5+ Kg8 32 Bxg6 Black resigned

32...Bxg6 allows 33 Qg7 mate.

Game 26
□ **Brodsky** ■ **Kramnik**
Herson 1991

1 e4 c5 2 Nf3 Nc6 3 d4 cxd4 4 Nxd4 Nf6 5 Nc3 e5 6 Ndb5 d6 7 Bg5 a6 8 Na3 b5 9 Bxf6 gxf6 10 Nd5 f5 11 Bd3

Traditionally this move has been the main line, but in the last few years it has been slowly ousted by 11 c3.

11...Be6 12 Qh5!?

Real aggression. The more subdued way of playing is with 12 0-0, after which Black normally eliminates White's knight with 12...Bxd5 13 exd5 Ne7.

12...Rg8!

Typically uncompromising play. Black develops his rook along the half-open g-file and attacks the g2-pawn, but leaves h7 unguarded. The safer approach is with 12...Bg7 13 0-0 f4, followed by ...0-0 (but not 13...0-0?? 14 exf5 Bxd5 15 f6!).

TIP: Rooks love open lines!

13 0-0-0!?

White places his king into relative safety, although it doesn't look so safe in a few moves time!

13...Rxg2 14 f4?

This move allows Black to take the initiative. 14 Qf3!, with a very unclear position, was the way forward.

14...Nd4! 15 Ne3 Rf2 16 exf5 Bxa2

Nibbling away at White's defences and crucially taking away the b1-square from the white king. This is very important in the oncoming tactics.

17 fxe5 dxe5 18 Nxb5 (Diagram 6)

White finds a way to sacrifice his dormant knight on a3, but Kramnik's reply is truly staggering.

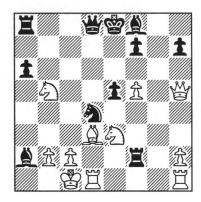

Diagram 6	**Diagram 7**
Black's next move is unbelievable	Black's pieces are having a party!

18...Bh6!!

Pinning the knight on e3 to the white king, but surely this bishop can be captured?

19 Rhe1

Apparently not! 19 Qxh6 Rxc2+!! mates after 20 Bxc2 Ne2 or 20 Nxc2 Nb3.

19...axb5! 20 Bxb5+ Ke7 21 Qh4+

21 Qxh6 again allows a combination: 21...Rxc2+! 22 Nxc2 Nb3 mate.

21...f6 22 Qxf2 Bf7

White is material up but it's Black who has the attack. Furthermore, the pin along the long h6-c1 diagonal is devastatingly effective.

23 Bd3 Qb6 24 Be4 Ra2 25 c4 Bxc4 26 Kb1

Finally the pin is broken, but Black's attack is just too powerful.

26...Qa5 (Diagram 7)

Black threatens ...Ra1 mate. There is no good defence. For example: 27 Nc2 Ra1+! 28 Nxa1 Qa2 mate.

27 Nd5+ Bxd5 28 Qxd4 Ra1+ 29 Kc2 Rxd1 30 Qxd1 Qa4+ 31 Kc3 White resigned

Black's next move is 31...Qc4 mate. This is one of the most famous Sveshnikov games of all time.

White plays 9 Nd5

1 e4 c5 2 Nf3 Nc6 3 d4 cxd4 4 Nxd4 Nf6 5 Nc3 e5 6 Ndb5 d6 7 Bg5 a6 8 Na3 b5 9 Nd5

Instead of capturing on f6, White intensifies the pin by moving the knight to d5. This is the main alternative to 9 Bxf6.

9...Be7

Breaking the pin and forcing White to reveal his hand.

9...Qa5+!? 10 Bd2 Qd8 is a cheeky idea, challenging White to find something better than just to repeat moves with 11 Bg5. If White is looking for more than a quick draw then he can play 11 Nxf6+ or enter the complications of 11 c4!?.

10 Bxf6

The most logical choice. White keeps the powerful knight on d5.

10...Bxf6 11 c3

Once again White aims to regroup his worst placed piece.

11...0-0 12 Nc2

The knight is once again heading for e3, where it supports the other knight on d5. Also, by vacating the a3-square, White paves the way to strike on the queenside with an early a2-a4

12...Bg5

A useful move. Black relocates his traditionally 'bad' bishop so that it has the opportunity to exchange itself for the knight when it reaches the e3-square. Another positive feature of this move is that it prepares an eventual pawn break with ...f7-f5 (possibly supported by ...g7-g6).

The move 12...Rb8 is seen in Game 28.

NOTE: A 'bad' bishop is one which is blocked by its own pawns.

13 a4

Attacking the black pawn structure on the queenside and bringing the a1-rook into the game. 13 Be2 followed by 0-0 is a less aggressive way to play the position.

NOTE: The move a2-a4 is a common attacking tool for White in the Sveshnikov.

13...bxa4

The simplest solution to the problem of the attacked pawn. 13...Rb8 14 axb5 axb5 gives White the a-file and leaves the isolated b-pawn very vulnerable.

14 Rxa4 a5 (Diagram 8)

This pawn is easier to defend on a5 and Black can now consider activating his own queenside rook with ...Rb8.

Diagram 8
A typical position from the 9 Nd5 variation

Strategies

It's fair to say that 9 Nd5 usually leads to quieter and more strategical positions than 9 Bxf6. In Diagram 8 White will complete development before trying to exploit his better pawn structure. White is actively placed on the queenside and often seeks to create a dangerous passed pawn on this wing with b2-b4.

Black's counterplay is once again based on kingside operations. The usual pawn break is ...f7-f5, often supported by ...g7-g6. The game often hinges on the respective speeds of Black's and White's attacks on the opposite wings.

Theoretical?

9 Nd5 is less theoretical than 9 Bxf6 and Black is less likely to get wiped off the board if he is unsure of the correct move-orders.

Statistics

9 Nd5 is very similar in the popularity stakes to 9 Bxf6. I found just over 6,000 games in *Mega Database 2002*, with White scoring a lower-than-average 51%. The positional nature of this line is reflected in the number of decisive games, which at 62% is lower than average and especially low for the Sveshnikov.

Illustrative Games

Game 27
□ **Lutz** ■ **Kramnik**
German Bundesliga 1995

1 e4 c5 2 Nf3 Nc6 3 d4 cxd4 4 Nxd4 Nf6 5 Nc3 e5 6 Ndb5 d6 7 Bg5 a6 8 Na3 b5 9 Nd5 Be7 10 Bxf6 Bxf6 11 c3 0-0 12 Nc2 Bg5 13 a4 bxa4 14 Rxa4 a5 15 Bc4

White sensibly develops his light-squared bishop and gets ready to castle.

15...Rb8

A typical Sveshnikov move, activating the rook and attacking the b2-pawn.

16 b3 Kh8 17 0-0 g6!?

Kramnik prefers to support the ...f7-f5 advance with his g-pawn. The other possibility is the immediate 17...f5.

18 Qe2 Bd7

A useful move, which indirectly hits the rook on a4.

19 Rfa1 Bh6

Now the queen can come out to the active h4-post. White's next move prevents this.

20 g3 f5!

Finally this lunge comes.

21 exf5?!

This is too accommodating. White should begin queenside operations with 21 b4!.

21...gxf5 22 b4 e4!

Now the knight is coming to e5 and Black's pieces are beginning to look menacing.

23 bxa5?

In his note to the game Kramnik prefers giving up an exchange with 23 Rxa5! Nxa5 24 Rxa5, when at least White no longer has to worry about ...Ne5 ideas.

23...Ne5 24 Rb4 Rxb4 25 cxb4 (Diagram 9)

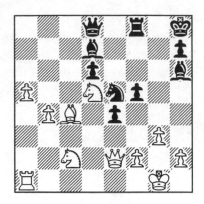

Diagram 9
White's kingside needs urgent attention

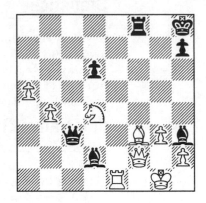

Diagram 10
Black's bishops have the final say.

If White had more time these pawns on the queenside would be winners, but Kramnik is going to break through on the kingside first.

25...f4! 26 Nd4

Exercise 4: What does Black play after 26 Qxe4 here?

26...e3!

Black marches on!

27 fxe3 f3! 28 Qa2 f2+ 29 Kg2

Or 29 Kh1 Nxc4 30 Qxc4 Bh3 31 Nf4 Qa8+! 32 Nc6 f1Q+ 33 Rxf1 Bxf1 and Black wins.

29...Qe8!

Now all of Black's remaining pieces are participating in the attack. There is no way for White to defend successfully.

30 Be2 Ng4 31 Bf3 Nxe3+ 32 Nxe3 Qxe3! 33 Qxf2 Bh3+! 34 Kg1 Qc3

Threatening both ...Qxa1+ and ...Be3.

35 Re1 Bd2! (Diagram 10) White resigns

White loses material, for example: 36 Nb5 Qxf3, 36 Re4 Qc1+, or 36 Rd1 Be3.

Game 28
□ **Kasparov** ■ **Lautier**
Moscow Olympiad 1994

---

1 e4 c5 2 Nf3 e6 3 d4 cxd4 4 Nxd4 Nf6 5 Nc3 Nc6 6 Ndb5 d6 7 Bf4 e5 8 Bg5 a6 9 Na3 b5 10 Nd5 Be7 11 Bxf6 Bxf6 12 c3 0-0 13 Nc2 Rb8

With this move Black takes prophylactic measures on the queenside and dissuades White from playing a2-a4. After 14 a4 bxa4! the black rook attacks b2-pawn.

14 h4!? (Diagram 11)

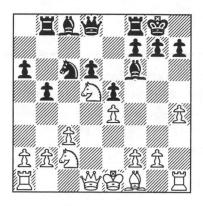
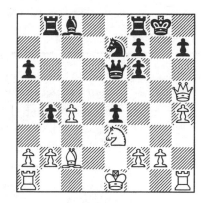

Diagram 11
What's the big idea?

Diagram 12
Only White is attacking

So Kasparov strikes on the other side of the board! This move is actually positionally motivated – it prevents Black from playing the desirable ...Bg5. Of course White could play more quietly with 14 Bc2 or 14 Bd3, but then this has never been Kasparov's style.

NOTE: White often delays castling in the Sveshnikov.

14...Ne7

Challenging the knight on d5, and preparing to accept doubled f-pawns again. Note that 14...Bxh4?? is a suicidal pawn grab; after 15 Qh5 Black will lose the bishop on h4.

15 Nxf6+ gxf6 16 Bd3!? d5

Black has won the battle of the d5-square but at some price: his king is weakened and will be subjected to a typical Kasparov onslaught.

17 exd5 Qxd5 18 Ne3 Qe6 19 Qh5 e4?!

Kasparov preferred 19...f5 20 0-0-0 Qg6 21 Qg5 f6 22 Qxg6+ hxg6 23 Bc2 and White is only slightly better.

20 Bc2 b4?! 21 c4! (Diagram 12)

Closing an avenue of black counterplay.

21...Kh8 22 0-0-0 f5 23 Qg5 Rb6 24 h5 Rc6 25 Kb1 Rc5 26 h6

Threatening an obvious mate in one on g7, but White also has other attacking ideas...

26...Qe5

26...Rg8 27 Rd8! is very strong for White.

27 Rh5! Rg8

An example of the tactics favouring White is 27...Nc6 28 Ng4 fxg4 29 Qg7+! Qxg7 30 hxg7+ Kxg7 31 Rxc5 and White has won material.

28 Ng4! Black resigns

A pretty finish. Black loses after either 28...Rxg5 29 Nxe5 Rxh5 30 Rd8+ Ng8 31 Nxf7 mate, or 28...Qe6 29 Rd8 Qg6 30 Qxe7 fxg4 31 Rxg8+ Qxg8 32 Qf6+.

Summary

1) The Sveshnikov is different to many Sicilian lines in that Black accepts structural weaknesses in return for active play.

2) White should follow the main lines with 6 Ndb5, as alternatives present Black with a very comfortable position.

3) The 9 Bxf6 line usually leads to very sharp play and is well suited to tactical players.

4) In contrast, the 9 Nd5 line is quieter and more suited to positional players.

Chapter Five

The Classical Variation

1 e4 c5 2 Nf3 d6 3 d4 cxd4 4 Nxd4 Nf6 5 Nc3 Nc6

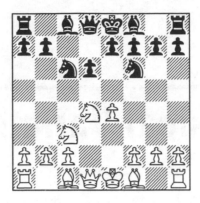

Diagram 1
The starting position for the Classical Variation

Despite being around for well over a century, this line of the Sicilian was for a very long time 'the variation with no name'. Then the English Grandmaster John Nunn christened it 'the Classical' in the first edition of his famous *Beating the Sicilian* book and this name seems to have stuck. The word 'classical' refers to Black's very normal 'Sicilian style' development. Both knights have reached their most natural posts and Black keeps his options open as to how the rest of his army will develop. Depending on how White acts, Black may react with ...e7-e6, ...e7-e5 or ...g7-g6. Sometimes the Classical simply transposes into variations we've already covered and I'll strive to point out the occasions when Black has the option to do this.

The Classical Variation is a solid and dependable choice for Black and has been used at the highest level by players such as Kramnik and Anand. One of its appeals is that on the whole it's slightly less theoretical than the Najdorf and the Dragon and so it requires less learning from the black player.

The Richter-Rauzer Attack

1 e4 c5 2 Nf3 d6 3 d4 cxd4 4 Nxd4 Nf6 5 Nc3 Nc6 6 Bg5 (Diagram 2)

The Richter-Rauzer Attack is White's most popular choice against the Classical. As with 6 Bg5 against the Najdorf, White develops his c1-bishop early in preparation of queenside castling.

6...e6

The normal move. Black prepares to develop his kingside bishop.

If Black tries to transpose into a Dragon Variation with 6...g6?!, then he finds his pawn structure ruined after 7 Bxf6! exf6. Also not to be recommended is the move 6...e5?!. After 7 Bxf6 Black is already in some bother: 7...Qxf6? 8 Nd5! Qd8 9 Nb5! gives White a winning position as early as move nine while 7...gxf6 8 Nf5 gives Black a structure similar to the one he obtains in the Sveshnikov, the major difference being that white's knight is on a wonderful outpost on f5 rather than the horrible a3-square he is forced to in the Sveshnikov.

Diagram 2
The Richter-Rauzer Attack

Diagram 3
A typical Richter-Rauzer position

The move 6...Bd7, however, is playable. White should probably continue as normal with 7 Qd2.

7 Qd2

Preparing to castle queenside.

7...a6

Again we see this typical little move. Black prevents a white piece coming to b5 and also prepares later queenside action with ...b7-b5.

Kingside development is also possible. For the move 7...Be7, see Game 30.

8 0-0-0 h6

Asking the question to the bishop on g5. Black can also develop on the queenside with 8...Bd7 (see Game 31).

9 Be3

Another way to play is with 9 Bf4, putting early pressure on the d6-pawn. Now 9...Nxd4?! 10 Qxd4 e5? would be a mistake on account of 11 Bxe5!. Instead Black can continue with 9...Bd7. Following 10 Nxc6 Bxc6, White cannot win a pawn with 11 Bxd6 as Black regains it after 11...Bxd6 12 Qxd6 Qxd6 13 Rxd6 Bxe4. Instead White normally opts to protect the e4-pawn with 11 f3.

Also possible is the natural retreat 9 Bh4, although this allows Black to win a pawn with the trick 9...Nxe4!. Now both 10 Bxd8 Nxd2 and 10 Nxe4 Qxh4 are fine for Black, so White should try 10 Qf4 Ng5 with a little compensation for the pawn.

9...Be7 10 f4 Nxd4

The immediate ...b7-b5 lunge leaves the knight en prise on c6, so Black exchanges knights first.

11 Bxd4 b5 (Diagram 3)

Strategies

In Diagram 3 Black has a typically resilient Sicilian structure and White must try to use his lead in development to drum up an initiative or else he could easily wind up being worse. Black will strive to complete development while keeping an eye on all of White's attacking ideas. Black has to be particularly wary of the e4-e5 pawn break.

Theoretical?

Black has quite a few different ways of playing against the Richter-Rauzer so if anything it's more difficult for White to learn than Black (assuming Black is simply content to learn just one defence). The Richter-Rauzer is less critical than, say, the Bg5 Najdorf or the Yugoslav Attack against the Dragon in that one small mistake is less likely to have a decisive effect on the game.

Statistics

As I mentioned before, the Richter-Rauzer is White's most popular answer to the Classical. White's moves are natural and he plays with less risk than in the Sozin and Velimirovic Attacks (see later). I found over 12,000 examples of the Richter-Rauzer in *Mega Database 2002*. White scores just below average with 53%, while 65% of the games were decisive.

Illustrative Games

Game 29
□ Ivanchuk ■ Kramnik
Dos Hermanas 1996

1 e4 c5 2 Nf3 Nc6

In the Classical the moves ...d7-d6 and ...Nc6 are interchangeable. Here Kramnik adopts the 2...Nc6 move order.

3 d4 cxd4 4 Nxd4 Nf6 5 Nc3 d6 6 Bg5 e6 7 Qd2 a6 8 0-0-0 h6 9 Be3 Be7 10 f4 Nxd4 11 Bxd4 b5 12 Qe3

White moves his queen off the d-file and sets up the idea of e4-e5. Alternatives include 12 Kb1, 12 Be2 and 12 Bd3.

12...Qc7

Removing the queen from the d-file, thus taking some of the sting out of e4-e5.

13 e5 dxe5 14 Bxe5 (Diagram 4)

14 fxe5 is a major alternative, to which Black should reply 14...Nd7.

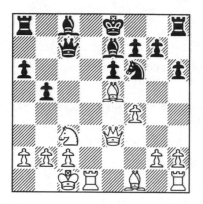

Diagram 4
Black must move his queen, right?

Diagram 5
White's defences have disintegrated

14...Ng4!

This move caused a major reassessment of this line. Previously Black has simply moved his queen away, but this counter-attack looks promising.

15 Qf3

Attacking both the rook on a8 and the knight on g4. Black must give up material.

NOTE: There are many tactical possibilities for White in the Sicilian involving the unprotected rook on a8.

15...Nxe5 16 Qxa8 Nd7 17 g3?

After this move White gets into a bit of a tangle. Kramnik suggests 17 Qf3 as a stronger try.

17...Nb6 18 Qf3 Bb7 19 Ne4

The only move, otherwise the rook on h1 would be lost.

19...f5! 20 Qh5+ Kf8 21 Nf2 Bf6!

Black can win back the exchange with 21...Bxh1 but Kramnik prefers to keep his bishops for attacking purposes.

22 Bd3 Na4! 23 Rhe1

Exercise 5: What should Black play after 23 c3?

23...Bxb2+ 24 Kb1 Bd5!

It's interesting that Kramnik doesn't require his rook on h8 to participate in the attack. The queen and three minor pieces cause enough trouble on their own.

25 Bxb5! Bxa2+!

25...axb5? 26 Rxd5! saves White as 26...exd5?? allows 27 Re8 mate.

26 Kxa2 axb5 27 Kb1 Qa5?!

A mistake in time trouble. In his notes in *Informator*, Kramnik gives the winning sequence 27...Qe7! 28 Rd3 Qb4! 29 Rd8+ Ke7 30 Re8+ Rxe8 31 Rxe6+ Kxe6 32 Qxe8+ Kf6 33 Qd8+ Kg6 and White runs out of checks.

28 Nd3? (Diagram 5)

28 c3! was White's only chance to stay alive.

28...Ba3!

Now the attack is too much for White to handle. Black threatens the deadly 29...Nc3+ 30 Ka1 Bc1 mate!

29 Ka2 Nc3+ 30 Kb3 Nd5 31 Ka2

Or 31 Rxe6 Qa4+ 32 Ka2 Nc3+ 33 Ka1 Bc1 mate.

31...Bb4+ 32 Kb1 Bc3 White resigns

Black forces mate after 33 Nb2 Qa3.

Game 30
□ **Oll** ■ **Hodgson**
Groningen 1993

---

1 e4 c5 2 Nf3 d6 3 d4 cxd4 4 Nxd4 Nf6 5 Nc3 Nc6 6 Bg5 e6 7 Qd2 Be7

With this move Black concentrates on developing and castling before trying to find active counterplay on the queenside.

8 0-0-0 0-0 9 f4

The most popular move; White gains further control over the centre.

The move 9 Bxf6 looks on first sight as if it forces Black to recapture with the g-pawn, but Black can actually continue with 9...Bxf6! 10 Nxc6 bxc6 11 Qxd6 Qb6 when Black's activity compensates for the loss of the d-pawn. Another direct attempt to exploit the 'weakness' of the d-pawn (along with the fact that Black has omitted...a7-a6) is with 9 Ndb5. Again Black can sacrifice the pawn for an active game: 9...Qa5! 10 Bxf6 Bxf6 11 Nxd6 Rd8 and the pin on the d-file is a bit awkward for White.

Finally, White can also try 9 Nb3 again with pressure on d6. One way for Black to combat this is to play 9...Qb6 10 f3 (or 10 Bxf6 Bxf6 11 Na4 Qc7 and now grabbing the pawn loses after 12 Qxd6?? Bg5+ 13 Kb1 Rd8!) 10...Rd8 and d6 is securely defended.

TIP: Look for ways to sacrifice the d6-pawn in return for active play.

9...Nxd4

Black exchanges in the centre in an attempt to free his position. Another main line runs 9...h6 10 Bh4 (10 Bxf6 Bxf6 11 Nxc6 bxc6 12 Qxd6 Qb6 again gives Black good activity for the pawn) 10...e5 11 Nf5 Bxf5 12 exf5.

10 Qxd4 Qa5

The first sign of counterplay. Black's queen is activated on the queen-side.

11 Bc4 Bd7 12 e5

On first sight this move looks very strong, but Black can rely on a useful trick to hold everything together. If White is reluctant to enter this forcing sequence he could try 12 Rhe1 or 12 Kb1.

12...dxe5 13 fxe5

If the knight moves the bishop on d7 will be en prise. What should Black do?

13...Bc6!

This calm move is the answer. The e5-pawn is pinned along the fifth rank, so 14 exf6 can be answered by 14...Qxg5+.

14 Bd2

The bishop retreats to safety. Now the threat on f6 is real.

14...Nd7 15 Nd5

Using a discovered attack on the black queen, White is able to trade his knight for Black's dark-squared bishop.

15...Qc5 16 Nxe7+ Qxe7 17 Rhe1 Rfd8 18 Qg4 Nf8 19 Bd3 Rxd3!?

An interesting exchange sacrifice, which has been tried quite a few times in this line (we are still deep in theory!). Black eliminates White's light-squared bishop so that his own bishop on c6 can rule the light squares. 19...Rd5 is a less committal way to play.

20 cxd3 Qd7 21 Kb1

Most theoreticians agree that 21 Bb4! gives White more chance of keeping an advantage.

21...Qxd3+ 22 Ka1 h5!

Deflecting the white queen.

23 Qxh5?

23 Qe2 is stronger.

23...Ba4! 24 Bc3

24 b3 Qd4+ 25 Kb1 Bb5 gives Black a strong attack, for example: 26 a4 Bd3+ 27 Ka2 Bc2 28 Rf1 Ng6 and Black wins back some material.

24...Bxd1 25 Rxd1 Qe4 26 Qg5 a5 27 Qd2 Ng6 28 g3 Ne7 29 Qd7 Nd5 30 Bd4 Qe2 31 Rc1! b5 32 Bc5 Qd3 33 Qc6 Rd8 34 Bd6 (Diagram 6)

34...Kh7!!

Using great imagination, Hodgson intends to activate his rook via h8!

35 Qc5 Kg6 36 h4 Rh8! 37 a3 Rh5 38 Qg1 Kh7 39 Rd1 Qb3 40 Rd2 Rf5

Finally Black's rook enters the game and this spells disaster for White.

41 g4 Rf4 42 Qb1+ Kg8 43 g5 b4! 44 Rd3 (Diagram 7)

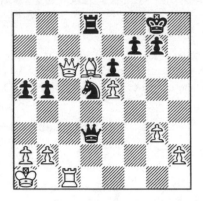

Diagram 6
How can Black activate his rook?

Diagram 7
Black to play and win!

44...Nc3! 45 Bxb4

45 bxc3 Qxa3+ 46 Qa2 Rf1+ mates.

45...Qa2+!! White resigns

A lovely finish to a fine game. Black mates after 46 Qxa2 Rf1+.

Game 31
□ **Adams** ■ **Kozul**
Belgrade 1999

---

1 e4 c5 2 Nf3 d6 3 d4 cxd4 4 Nxd4 Nf6 5 Nc3 Nc6 6 Bg5 e6 7 Qd2 a6 8 0-0-0 Bd7

Black protects his knight on c6 and plans an early ...b7-b5 thrust.

9 f4 b5 10 Bxf6!

Normally it's not a good idea to simply swap this bishop off for the knight, but on this occasion Black is forced to make a concession.

10...gxf6

10...Qxf6 looks natural but then 11 e5! is strong, the idea being that 11...dxe5 12 Ndxb5! uncovers a nasty attack on the bishop on d7.

11 Kb1 Qb6 12 Nxc6 Bxc6 13 Qe1!

A sneaky move. White plans to meet 13...b4 with 14 Nd5!, when 14...exd5 15 exd5+ regains the piece with a big advantage.

13...Be7 14 Bd3 a5 (Diagram 8)

Black slowly advances on the queenside, but perhaps Black should consider the immediate 14...b4.

15 f5!

An important move, putting pressure on the e6-pawn. If this pawn moves to e5 or captures on f5, then Black may well lose control of the crucial d5-square.

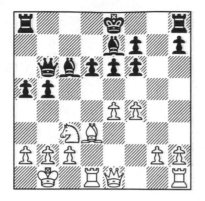

Diagram 8
What is White's plan?

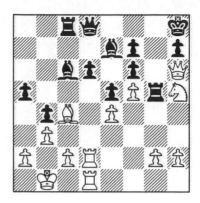

Diagram 9
White has total control

NOTE: The advance f2-f4-f5 can be particularly effective if Black has the doubled pawn complex f7/f6.

15...b4 16 Ne2 e5

Otherwise White simply captures on e6 and increases the pressure with Nf4 and Bc4.

17 Ng3 Qc5 18 Qe2

White wants to move his d3-bishop to c4, where it will be well placed along the long a2-g8 diagonal.

18...Rc8 19 b3 0-0 20 Bc4

White has achieved his objective and now has full control of the d5-square. Black is in for a grim struggle.

20...Kh8 21 Rhe1 Rg8

Adams suggests 21...a4 as a better way of gaining counterplay.

22 Qh5 Be8 23 Qh6 Qb6 24 Nh5 Qd8 25 Rd2 Rg5 26 Red1 Bc6 (Diagram 9)

White has slowly built up an attack and Black is reduced to severe passivity. Now comes the killer blow.

27 Nxf6!

This wins a crucial pawn and Black's position soon collapses.

27...Rg7 28 Nh5 Rg4 29 Nf6 Rg7 30 g4 Qb6 31 h3 Rd8 32 Nh5 Rgg8 33 Bxf7 Bg5 34 Qe6 Rgf8 35 Rxd6 Rxd6 36 Qxe5+ Rf6 37 Nxf6 Black resigns

The Sozin and Velimirovic Attacks

1 e4 c5 2 Nf3 d6 3 d4 cxd4 4 Nxd4 Nf6 5 Nc3 Nc6 6 Bc4 (Diagram 10)

Diagram 10
The Sozin Attack

Diagram 11
The Velimirovic Attack

This variation obtained its name from the Russian player Veniamin Sozin, who made a significant contribution to its theory in the 1930s. It has many similarities to the Fischer Attack against the Najdorf (see Chapter 2) and indeed Fischer adopted this variation too. The king's bishop is developed to an active post, pressurising the important a2-g8 diagonal.

6...e6

A natural response, sensibly blocking the path of the bishop. However, we should take a brief look at some alternatives:

a) 6...g6?!, trying to transpose into the Dragon Variation, allows White to play the sequence 7 Nxc6 bxc6 8 e5! and Black is forced to move the knight as 8...dxe5?? loses to the trick 9 Bxf7+! Kxf7 10 Qxd8.

b) 6...e5 is possible but many players are reluctant to leave the a2-g8 diagonal open. If Black wants to play this way, he should contest the diagonal as soon as possible with ...Be6.

c) 6...Qb6 is Black's most popular alternative to 6...e6 and is played by those unwilling to enter the complications of the Sozin or the Velimirovic Attack (see later). One possible continuation from here is 7 Nb3 e6 8 Be3 Qc7 9 0-0 a6 10 f4 Be7 11 Bd3 0-0 and we have reached a position that can also occur from the Scheveningen Variation.

 TIP: Be aware of possibilities of transposing into other Sicilian variations.

7 Be3

This is an aggressive indication that White will castle queenside. The older (Sozin) way to play is with kingside castling. After 7 0-0 Be7 8 Be3 0-0 9 Bb3 a6 10 f4 Nxd4 11 Bxd4 b5 a complex position has arisen with chances for both sides

7...a6 8 Qe2

We are now officially in the territory of the Velimirovic Attack, which was introduced by the Yugoslav Grandmaster Dragoljub Velimirovic in the 1960s.

8...Be7 9 0-0-0 0-0

Black can also delay or even do without castling. For 9...Qc7 see Game 33.

10 Bb3 Qc7 (Diagram 11)

Strategies

Play from Diagram 11 is particularly sharp as both sides attack on opposite flanks. One of White's main attacking weapons is the thrust g2-g4-g5, dislodging the black knight from its excellent defensive post on f6. Given time, White may continue the attack with moves such as Qh5 and Rhg1-g3-h3, while knight and bishop sacrifices are always on the cards especially on the d5-, e6- and f5-squares.

Black's counterplay once again lies on the queenside. This includes the thrust ...b7-b5-b4, displacing the c3-knight and thus adding pressure on White's slightly vulnerable e4-pawn. Time is of the essence and any dithering by either side is likely to be punished in the severest way.

Theoretical?

The Velimirovic rivals the Yugoslav Attack in the Dragon as one of the most theoretically complex lines of the Sicilian. Both players are advised to read up on the theory before embarking on the massive complications.

Statistics

Taking the position after 6 Bc4, I found over 8,000 examples in *Mega Database 2002*, with White scoring below average with 50%. Concentrating merely on the Velimirovic Attack (when White plays Qe2), there were over 2,000 examples, with White scoring 54%. The sharpness of the Velimirovic is illustrated by 73% ratio of decisive games.

Illustrative Games

Game 32
□ **Wolff** ■ **I.Sokolov**
Baguio City 1987

1 e4 c5 2 Nf3 e6 3 d4 cxd4 4 Nxd4 Nc6 5 Nc3 d6 6 Be3 Nf6 7 Bc4 Be7 8 Qe2 a6 9 0-0-0 Qc7 10 Bb3 0-0

The players adopted a different move order, but now we are at one of the major starting positions for the Velimirovic Attack.

11 Rhg1

White puts his rook behind the g-pawn to support its push. The immediate 11 g4 is the main alternative.

11...b5

Black begins counterplay on the queenside and prepares ...b5-b4.

12 g4 Na5

Another very complex line runs 12...b4 13 Nxc6 (13 Na4 will simply lose the e-pawn) 13...Qxc6 14 Nd5! exd5 15 g5 Nxe4 16 Bxd5 Qa4! with great complications.

13 g5 Nxb3+ 14 axb3 Nd7 15 f4 b4 (Diagram 12)

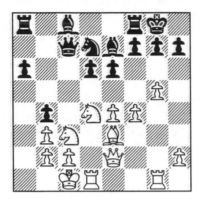

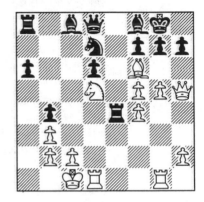

Diagram 12	**Diagram 13**
How should White proceed?	The bishop cannot be touched

16 Nf5!

We've already seen this type of sacrifice. White offers a piece to obtain control of the crucial d5-square

WARNING: When playing Black, beware of Nf5 sacrifices in the Velimirovic Attack.

16...exf5

This may well be a mistake! Black can decline the piece with 16...Nc5, for example: 17 Nxe7+ Qxe7 18 e5 bxc3 19 exd6 cxb2+ 20 Kxb2 Na4+! 21 bxa4 Qb7+ when White is a pawn up but his king looks a little vulnerable.

17 Nd5

Naturally the knight takes up its dominating position on d5.

17...Qd8 18 exf5 Re8 19 Bd4! Bf8

Two further examples illustrate how difficult Black's defensive task is here:

a) 19...Bb7 20 g6! fxg6 21 Qe6+ Kh8 22 Bxg7+! Kxg7 23 fxg6 Bxd5 24 Rxd5 Ne5 25 Rxe5 and Black resigned in Sarkar-Kolinko, Catonsville 2000.

b) 19...Bf6 20 Qxe8+! Qxe8 21 gxf6 g6 22 Ne7+ Kf8 and 23 Rd3! (with the idea of Rh3) gave White an awesome attack in Nijboer-Winants, Wijk aan Zee 1988.

20 Qh5 Re4 21 Bf6! (Diagram 13)

21...Qe8

The bishop is immune from attack. White mates after 21...gxf6 22 Nxf6+ Nxf6 23 gxf6+ Kh8 24 Qg5.

22 Nc7 Nxf6 23 gxf6 Qd8 24 Nd5 Bb7 25 fxg7 Be7

25...Bxg7 loses to 26 f6.

26 Rg3 Bf6 27 Rh3 Bxg7 28 Qxh7+ Kf8 29 f6

Even stronger is 29 Qxg7+! Kxg7 30 Rg1+ Kf8 31 Rh8 mate!

29...Bxf6 30 Qxe4 Qa5 31 Qf5 Bg7 32 Qd7 Black resigns

After 32...Bxd5 33 Qxd6+ Kg8 34 Qxd5 White wins easily.

Game 33
□ **Emms** ■ **Hennigan**
British Ch., Dundee 1993

1 e4 c5 2 Nf3 Nc6 3 d4 cxd4 4 Nxd4 Nf6 5 Nc3 d6 6 Bc4 e6 7 Be3 Be7 8 Qe2 a6 9 0-0-0 Qc7 10 Bb3 Na5

Here Black delays castling which gives him an extra tempo for queen-side operations.

11 g4 b5 12 g5 Nxb3+ 13 axb3 Nd7 14 h4

Pressing forward on the kingside. Another main line is 14 Nf5!? (that move again) 14...exf5 15 Nd5 Qd8 16 exf5 and again White has good compensation for the piece.

14...b4 15 Na4 Nc5 (Diagram 14)

16 h5!?

It's tempting to attack in this caveman manner, but there is also something to be said about simply defending the e4-pawn with 16 f3. After Black grabs on e4 the onus is on White to produce something special, otherwise he has simply lost a crucial central pawn.

TIP: Always think carefully before sacrificing a crucial central pawn.

16...Nxe4!?

16...Bd7 is more common, but there seems to be nothing wrong with this natural capture.

17 g6 Bf6!

My opponent had analysed this position before the game and had come to the conclusion that it's fully playable for Black. Now I agree with him!

18 gxf7+ Kxf7 19 Rhg1?

This move is too pedestrian. 19 Bf4 causes Black more problems.

19...e5! 20 Nf3 Bf5 21 Kb1 Rab8

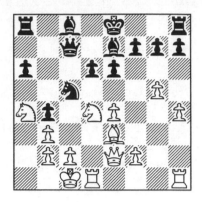

Diagram 14
Should White protect the e4-pawn?

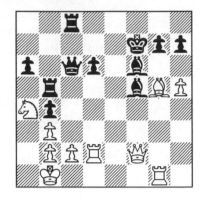

Diagram 15
The c2-pawn is vulnerable

Now Black is fully developed and White has very little to show for the pawn deficit.

22 Nd2 Nxd2+ 23 Rxd2 Rhc8 24 f4 Rb5 25 Qf2 exf4 26 Bxf4 Qc6 27 Bg5 (Diagram 15) 27...Qxc2+!

This move simplifies the position into a winning endgame for Black.

28 Rxc2

28 Ka2 is met by 28...Qxb3+!! 29 Kxb3 Be6+ 30 Rd5 Bxd5 mate!

28...Rxc2 29 Qxf5 Rxf5 30 Bxf6 Rcf2! 31 Bd8 Rf1+ 32 Rxf1 Rxf1+ 33 Kc2 Rh1 34 Ba5 Rxh5 35 Bxb4 Ke6 36 Bd2 g5

These kingside pawns will be too powerful for White.

37 Nc3 g4 38 Kd3 Rh2 39 Ke3 h5 40 Ne4 d5 41 Nc5+ Kf5 42 Bc3 h4 43 Nd3 Rh3+ White resigns

44 Ke2 Rxd3! 45 Kxd3 h3 and the h-pawn promotes.

The Boleslavsky Variation

1 e4 c5 2 Nf3 d6 3 d4 cxd4 4 Nxd4 Nf6 5 Nc3 Nc6 6 Be2 e5 (Diagram 16)

The Boleslavsky Variation has many similarities to 6 Be2 e5 variation of the Najdorf (see Chapter 2). Black pushes his e-pawn and forces White's knight to move from its central post.

I should point out that Black has two transpositional moves against 6 Be2: the move 6...g6 will move us into Dragon territory (see Chapter 1), while 6...e6 gives us a Classical Scheveningen (see Chapter 3).

7 Nf3

After 7 Nb3 Be7 8 0-0 0-0 we get very similar play to the 6 Be2 e5 variation of the Najdorf. Here Black's knight is committed to c6, but on the other hand Black can save time by omitting the move ...a7-a6.

One possible continuation is 9 Kh1 a5!? (with the idea of ...a5-a4) 10 a4 Nb4 and Black's knight has a useful outpost on b4.

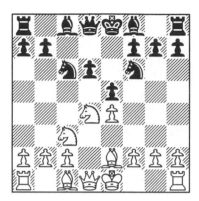

Diagram 16	**Diagram 17**
The Boleslavsky Variation	White prevents ...d6-d5

7...h6

The most popular choice. The immediate 7...Be7 is also very playable, but with 7...h6 Black prevents any white ideas of playing Bg5, Bxf6 and Nd5.

8 0-0 Be7 9 Re1

At first sight this move looks a little strange, but there is good reason for it. White can really only hope to keep an advantage if he prevents Black from playing the typical freeing advance ...d6-d5. The one reasonable way to this here is to put pressure on the e5-pawn, thus dissuading Black from carrying out the advance. All will become clearer in another couple of moves!

9...0-0 10 h3

Another prophylactic move, preventing ...Bg4.

10...Be6

Preparing the desirable ...d6-d5.

11 Bf1! (Diagram 17)

Just in time! White prevents ...d6-d5, which would now lose a pawn after 11...d5 12 exd5 Nxd5 13 Nxd5 Bxd5 14 Nxe5. Now Black has to look elsewhere for counterplay.

Strategies

Once again the battle for the d5-square is one of the key issues in this line. If Black is allowed to play ...d6-d5 then usually all his problems are over and White's are just starting. If White can prevent this advance, then sometimes Black is driven to a state of passivity. Sometimes White will play Nd5 and after an exchange a new pawn structure will be formed with a white pawn on d5. Play is much quieter and there are often lengthy manoeuvres by each side

Theoretical?

Given the generally quiet nature of this position, this line is much less theoretical than the Richter-Rauzer, the Sozin and the Velimirovic Attacks and appeals to the more positionally minded player.

Statistics

I found nearly 3,000 examples of 6 Be2 e5 in *Mega Database 2002*. White scores a pretty dismal 43%, while 65% of the games are decisive. White's low score can be partially explained by the fact that the average rating of those playing black was higher, but this still seems to suggest that that 6 Be2 e5 is a comfortable system for Black.

Illustrative Games

Game 34
□ **Womacka** ■ **Aseev**
Germany 1991

1 e4 c5 2 Nf3 d6 3 d4 cxd4 4 Nxd4 Nf6 5 Nc3 Nc6 6 Be2 e5 7 Nf3 h6 8 0-0 Be7 9 Re1 0-0 10 h3 Be6 11 Bf1 Nb8

An interesting idea. Black takes some time out to manoeuvre the knight to a stronger square. The most natural alternative is 11...Rc8.

NOTE: In quiet positions, a loss of time is not so important.

12 b3 a6 13 Bb2 Nbd7 14 a4!

Preventing Black from playing ...b7-b5.

14...Qc7 (Diagram 18)

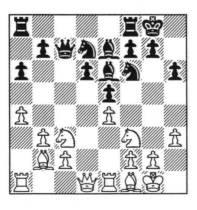

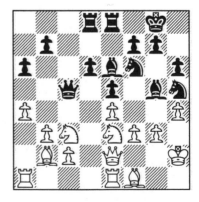

| **Diagram 18** | **Diagram 19** |
| Slow manoeuvring is the key | White has kingside weaknesses |

15 Nd2!

A good idea. White plans to manoeuvre the knight to e3, where it aims at the crucial d5-square. See the similarity between this plan and Karpov's Nb3-c1-a2-b4 in Game 16.

15...Rad8 16 Nc4 Rfe8 17 Ne3 Qc6 18 f3?!

But this move is an unjustified weakening of the kingside. 18 Qf3! would have kept a small advantage for White.

18...Qc5! 19 Kh2 Nh5!

Black plans ...Bh4. Suddenly White has trouble protecting his weak dark squares on the kingside.

20 g3 Bg5 21 Qe2 Ndf6

Black goes for an all out assault on the white king.

22 h4?! (Diagram 19)

This is just asking for a sacrifice to be made.

22...Nxg3! 23 Kxg3 Nh5+ 24 Kh2 Bxh4 25 Red1 Bg3+ 26 Kg1 Nf4 27 Qd2

White's kingside has disintegrated and now Black can push through with a thematic central advance.

27...d5! 28 Ba3 Qa7 29 exd5 Bxd5 30 Ncxd5 Nxd5 31 Bc1 Bf4 32 Re1 e4

Another breakthrough. Note that the immediate 32...Nxe3?? allows White to play 33 Qf2, pinning and winning the knight on e3.

33 Qf2 exf3 34 Nxd5 Bh2+! White resigns

The queen on f2 is lost.

Summary

1) The Classical Variation is a reliable defence for Black. It's easy to play and there are less lines to learn than, say, in the Dragon or the Najdorf.

2) The Richter-Rauzer Attack is White's most popular response, although Black has quite a wide choice of reactions to this line.

3) The Velimirovic Attack is the sharpest line of the Classical. Black may, if he wishes, avoid all the complexities by choosing 6...Qb6.

4) As with many other variations, 6 Be2 leads to quieter play and is more suitable for positional players.

Chapter Six

Other Open Sicilians

The Taimanov Variation

1 e4 c5 2 Nf3 e6 3 d4 cxd4 4 Nxd4 Nc6 (Diagram 1)

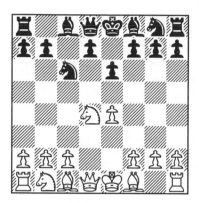

Diagram 1
The Taimanov Variation

This line of the Sicilian has been named after the Soviet Grandmaster Mark Taimanov, who has played hundreds of games and developed many of the systems. Black's pawn formation is flexible and play can sometimes transpose into the Scheveningen if Black plays an early ...d7-d6. However, Black often keeps a Taimanov flavour by leaving the d-pawn at home so that the f8-bishop may be actively developed along the f8-a3 diagonal. Black sometimes develops the other bishop on b7 after an introductory ...a7-a6 and ...b7-b5.

5 Nc3

White develops in normal fashion. Another major possibility for White here is 5 Nb5 (see Game 37).

5...Qc7

This little queen move is a characteristic of the variation. On c7 the queen controls the long b8-h2 diagonal and may also influence events on the half-open c-file.

6 Be2

This is the main line of the Taimanov but White does have other options, including 6 Be3, 6 f4 and 6 g3. The move 6 Ndb5, attacking the black queen, is not as dangerous as it looks. Black replies with 6...Qb8! and later gains time on the knight with the advance ...a7-a6.

6...a6

Despite what I said above, Black does well to eliminate any possibility of Nb5 in the future. Of course, this move can also be a preliminary to queenside counterplay with ...b7-b5.

NOTE: Black hardly ever does without ...a7-a6 in the Taimanov.

7 Be3 Nf6

A further option for Black is to delay development on the kingside in favour of beginning operations on the other side: 7...b5 8 Nxc6 Qxc6 9 0-0 Bb7 10 Bf3 Rc8 and Black can continue development with ...Bc5 and ...Ne7.

8 0-0

Black now has the opportunity to transpose into the Classical Scheveningen after 8...Be7 9 f4 d6. In fact, this is the exact move order used in Game 23.

8...Bb4 (Diagram 2)

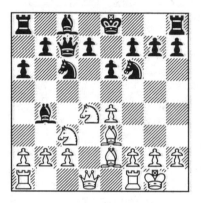

Diagram 2	Diagram 3
Black develops his king's bishop	Black is cramped but has an extra pawn

Keeping a Taimanov flavour to the game. Black develops the bishop to the active b4-post, putting pressure on White's e4-pawn by attacking its defender.

9 Na4!

This move looks a little strange at first. Isn't White leaving the crucial e4-pawn en prise? However, things are not so clear cut as there are many tactics favouring White.

In contrast, 9 f3?! is a little bit passive; 9...0-0, followed by ...d7-d5, gives Black a very comfortable game.

9...Be7

Having displaced the knight, the bishop returns to a safe home. Alternatives include:

a) 9...0-0 – see Game 36.

b) 9...Nxe4?! 10 Nxc6! Qxc6 (10...bxc6? 11 Qd4 forks two pieces) 11 Nb6 Rb8 12 Qd4 Bf8 13 Bf3 f5 14 Rad1 leaves Black a pawn up but with his position in a real mess. White has a powerful bind and Black will have great trouble completing his development.

10 c4!?

Again White offers a pawn sacrifice. This is the most aggressive way to play the position.

The other main choice is 10 Nxc6 bxc6 11 Nb6 Rb8 12 Nxc8 Qxc8, and now White can choose between 13 e5 and 13 Bd4.

10...Nxe4

Black can decline the sacrifice with 10...0-0, after which White can protect his e-pawn with 11 Nc3, or else push on with 11 c5. In the latter case, Black has nothing better than to grab the e4-pawn anyway.

11 c5

A crucial move, putting a significant cramping effect on Black's game. Black will now find it difficult to break with either ...b7-b5 or ...d7-d5.

11...0-0

Exercise 6: What happens after 11...Nxc5 here?

12 Rc1 (Diagram 3)

Supporting the forward c5-pawn.

Strategies

White can use his space advantage created by the pawn wedge on c5 to attack Black on either or both sides of the board. Black will find it difficult to free his position, but he must try. Eventually Black will probably opt for the advance ...d7-d6 (or ...d7-d5). When the position opens up, White's more active pieces will ensure that he keeps the initiative, but Black still has that extra pawn to cling on to.

Theoretical?

On the whole, the Taimanov is less theoretical than many of the other Sicilian variations, but a fair body of theory has built up on the in the main line leading to Diagram 3.

Statistics

The Taimanov has recently been growing in popularity, although it's fair to say that it's seen more commonly at international level than at club or tournament levels. Famous adherents include Vishy Anand and Judit Polgar. I found more than 17,000 examples of the Taimanov in *Mega Database 2002*, with Black scoring an impressive 50%.

Illustrative Games

Game 35
□ **Agnos** ■ **Miladinovic**
Greece 1998

1 e4 c5 2 Nf3 Nc6 3 d4 cxd4 4 Nxd4 Qc7 5 Nc3 e6 6 Be2 a6 7 0-0 Nf6 8 Be3 Bb4 9 Na4 Be7 10 c4 Nxe4 11 c5 0-0 12 Rc1 Rb8

A prophylactic move. The white knight may well be heading to b6, so the rook makes sure it won't be attacked when the knight gets there.

13 g3

Supporting a possible Bf4.

13...Kh8

Black tucks his king into safety. Complications arise after 13...f5 14 Bf4 e5 15 Nxf5! exf4 16 Qd5+ Kh8 17 Nxe7 Nxe7 18 Qxe4 d5 19 cxd6 Qxd6, although this final position looks pretty equal.

14 Bf3 f5

Supporting the attacked knight. The other option was to retreat with 14...Nf6, although in this case Black would remain very passive.

15 Bxe4 fxe4 16 Qc2?

After this move Black is able to break out of his bind. 16 Qg4!?, as suggested by Agnos, may be stronger. White will be able to round up Black's extra e4-pawn and 16...e5 can be answered by 17 Nf5!.

16...e5 17 Nb3 (Diagram 4)

17 Nxc6 dxc6! suddenly frees Black's c8-bishop. After 18 Qxe4 Bf5 19 Qb4 Bh3 20 Rfe1 Qd7 Black plans ...Qf5-f3.

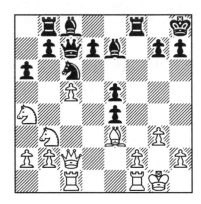

Diagram 4
Black must break out

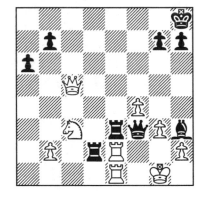

Diagram 5
Black can mate in two moves

17...d5!

Black must free his position.

18 cxd6 Qxd6 19 Bc5 Qf6 20 Qe2

20 Bxe7 Nxe7 21 Qxe4? loses material after 21...Bh3!.

20...Bh3 21 Rfe1 Nd4 22 Nxd4 exd4 23 Bxe7 Qxe7 24 Qxe4 Qf7!

White has finally won his pawn back but the position has been blown open. The light squares around White's own king are particularly weak and in the long run this proves to be decisive.

25 f4 Qxa2 26 Qxd4 Rbd8 27 Qb4 Qd5 28 Rc2 Rfe8! 29 Rce2

Re3!!

The beginning of a marvellous mating idea.

30 Nc3

Of course the rook cannot be taken: 30 Rxe3 allows 30...Qg2 mate.

30...Qf3 31 Qc4 Rd2!!

Now 32 Rxd2 Rxe1+ wins, but Black's last move also contained a devastating threat!

32 Qc5 (Diagram 5) 32...Qg2+! White resigns

A pleasing queen sacrifice to finish. It's checkmate after 33 Rxg2 Rxe1.

Game 36
☐ **Kuzmin** ■ **Sveshnikov**
Moscow 1973

---

1 e4 c5 2 Nf3 e6 3 d4 cxd4 4 Nxd4 Nc6 5 Nc3 Qc7 6 Be2 a6 7 0-0 Nf6 8 Be3 Bb4 9 Na4 0-0 10 Nxc6 bxc6 11 c4

Yet another pawn offer. The main alternative for White is 11 Nb6 Rb8 12 Nxc8 Rfxc8! 13 Bxa6 Rf8 and, despite being a pawn down, Black's position is okay. In fact, after 14 Bd3 Bd6! he wins the pawn back by force due to the double threat on h2 and b2. The game may continue 15 f4 e5! 16 f5 Rxb2 with a level position.

11...Bd6

Black moves the bishop to relative safety and gains an important tempo by attacking the h2-pawn. The immediate 11...Nxe4?! looks to be too risky. After 12 Qd4 Nf6 13 c5 Black's bishop is in great danger on b4, for example: 13...Nd5 14 a3 Ba5 15 b4 and the bishop is trapped.

12 f4 Nxe4 (Diagram 6)

Now it is much safer to grab the pawn, although White still achieves quite a strong initiative.

13 Bd3 Nf6 14 c5

Forcing the bishop back and gaining extra space on the queenside. Black is rather clamped, but he does have that crucial extra central pawn so White must do something quickly with his initiative.

14...Be7 15 Bd4

Now both bishops are pointing menacingly at the kingside.

15...Nd5??

It's true that the d5-square is attractive, but now Black suffers horribly by removing the knight from its defensive duties on the kingside. After 15...Rd8 Black would still be very much in the game.

WARNING: Always check carefully before moving away a crucial kingside defender.

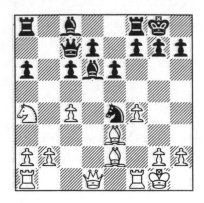

Diagram 6
Black grabs a pawn

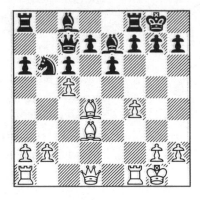

Diagram 7
One sacrifice follows another

16 Nb6!

First of all, White deflects the knight further away from the action.

16...Nxb6 (Diagram 7) 17 Bxh7+!

Now this sacrifice is decisive.

17...Kxh7

Black must capture; 17...Kh8 18 Qh5 mates very quickly.

18 Qh5+ Kg8 19 Bxg7!

Completely stripping the black king of its cover. This double bishop sacrifice is a well known theme.

19...Kxg7

Or 19...f6 20 Qg6 Bxc5+ 21 Kh1 and Black cannot avoid mate.

20 Qg4+ Kh7

20...Kf6 allows mate with 21 Qg5.

21 Rf3 Black resigns

The only way to avoid mate by Rh3 is with 21...Qd8, but then 22 Rh3+ Bh4 23 Rxh4+ Qxh4 24 Qxh4+ Kg7 25 cxb6 is easily winning for White.

Game 37
☐ **McShane** ■ **Plaskett**
Hastings 1997/98

---

1 e4 c5 2 Nf3 e6 3 d4 cxd4 4 Nxd4 Nc6 5 Nb5

As with the Sveshnikov, White highlights the weakness on the d6-square with this knight move.

5...d6

Logically, Black prevents Nd6+.

6 Bf4

Adding further pressure to the d6-pawn. After this move the position is reminiscent of the Sveshnikov Variation.

Another major option for White here is 6 c4, setting up the so called 'Maroczy Bind' (pawns on c4 and e4 restraining the black centre; we will see more of this bind in the Accelerated Dragon). Play can continue with 6...Nf6 7 N1c3 a6 8 Na3 Be7 9 Be2 0-0 10 0-0 b6 11 Be3 Bb7 and we see that Black has adopted the 'Hedgehog' formation (characterised by pawns on e6, d6, b6 and a6). The Maroczy Bind versus the Hedgehog is quite common in the Sicilian (it can also occur in the Kan Variation – see later on in this chapter). White has an obvious space advantage, but it's been shown through experience that Black's set-up is remarkably resilient. If White overpresses, he runs the risk of being impaled on one of the spikes!

6...e5

This move is virtually forced. Black must deal with the threat to his d-pawn.

7 Be3 Nf6

Good alternatives include 7...a6 and 7...Be6.

8 Bg5! (Diagram 8)

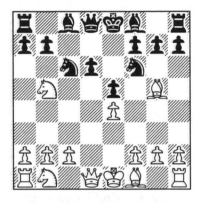
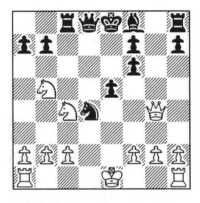

Diagram 8	**Diagram 9**
Has White lost a tempo?	White can win material

White's third move in a row with this piece, but somehow it all makes sense! The knight is pinned and thus the threat to the e-pawn is extinguished. If you look closely you will see that the position now very much resembles the Sveshnikov Variation 1 e4 c5 2 Nf3 Nc6 3 d4 cxd4 4 Nxd4 Nf6 5 Nc3 e5 6 Ndb5 d6 7 Bg5, the only difference being that White's knight is on b1 rather than c3. Normally you would think that this loss of time would be a disadvantage to White, but in this instance it's not so clear. One major plus factor is that the b5-knight can now retreat to c3 rather than the miserable a3-square.

8...Be6

Or 8...a6 9 Bxf6 gxf6 10 N5c3 and the queen's knight will develop via d2.

9 Bxf6 gxf6

This is forced; 9...Qxf6?? allows 10 Nc7+.

10 Nd2 d5?!

Normally this freeing advance would be good news for Black, but here the tactics work in White's favour. Stronger is the simple 10...a6 and Black is okay.

11 exd5 Bxd5 12 Bc4!

A powerful move, challenging Black's bishop in the centre.

12...Rc8

Alternatively:

a) 12...Bxg2 13 Rg1 gives White a very dangerous initiative, for example 13...Bh3 14 Qh5!.

b) 12...a6 13 Bxd5 axb5 14 Bb3 and Black has many pawn weakness with no redeeming features to his position, Leko-Portisch, Budapest 1997.

13 Qg4!

Now Black is in some trouble. White's most obvious threat is to capture on d5, as Black's rook on c8 will be left hanging.

13...Bxc4?

13...Nb4 is the only chance.

14 Nxc4

Now White simply has too many threats.

14...Nd4 (Diagram 9) 15 Nbd6+!

Winning an exchange.

15...Bxd6 16 Nxd6+ Ke7

Or 16...Qxd6 17 Qxc8+.

17 Nxc8+ Qxc8 18 Qxc8 Rxc8 19 Rc1 Rxc2 20 Rxc2 Nxc2+ 21 Kd2 Nb4 22 Rc1 Nc6 23 Rc3 Black resigns

White will continue with Rh3 and Rxh7.

The Accelerated Dragon

1 e4 c5 2 Nf3 Nc6 3 d4 cxd4 4 Nxd4 g6 (Diagram 10)

This variation is very closely linked to the Dragon in that the f8-bishop is fianchettoed along the h8-a1 diagonal, and often the two variations transpose into each other. The main difference is that Black chooses to fianchetto earlier and leaves his d7-pawn at home. In some variations this can prove to be advantageous to Black. We saw in the Dragon that Black often tried to engineer a ...d6-d5 break. In the Accelerated Dragon, Black can aim for an immediate ...d7-d5, thus effectively gaining an extra tempo. It's certainly within White's interests to prevent such an occurrence as this usually gives Black a very comfortable game.

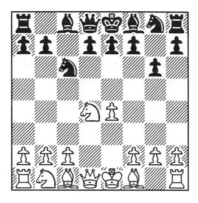

Diagram 10
The Accelerated Dragon

Diagram 11
A typical Accelerated Dragon

The main disadvantage the accelerated version has over the Dragon proper is that there is no early pressure on the e4-pawn with ...Nf6. This means that White can dispense with an early Nc3 and create the 'Maroczy Bind' with c2-c4. We've already seen how this bind can leave White with a lasting space advantage and how it virtually rules out the ...d7-d5 break. Nevertheless, the Accelerated Dragon is still a very solid option for Black, who keeps a resilient pawn structure.

NOTE: The Maroczy Bind makes it very difficult for Black to achieve the ...d6-d5 break.

5 c4

Setting up the Maroczy Bind. White now has a vice-like grip on the important d5-square.

For 5 Nc3, see Game 39.

5...Bg7 6 Be3

Protecting the knight on d4.

6...Nf6 7 Nc3 0-0

Another idea for Black is 7...Ng4!?, answering 8 Qxg4 with 8...Nxd4. Here White should deal with the double threat of ...Nc2+ and ...d7-d5 with 9 Qd1.

8 Be2 d6 9 0-0 Bd7

Black plans to exchange knights on d4 and then place this bishop on c6, attacking the e4-pawn.

10 Qd2 Nxd4 11 Bxd4 Bc6 12 f3 a5

Gaining space on the queenside. Black prepares to follow up with ...a5-a4 and ...Qa5.

13 b3

A prophylactic move. Now ...a5-a4 can be met by b3-b4 and it's White who gains space on the queenside.

13...Nd7

Offering the exchange of bishops.

14 Be3 (Diagram 11)

Of course, White could also capture on g7, but most experts agree that it's better to retain these bishops on the board.

Strategies

White will 'sit' with his space advantage, slowly waiting for a chance to create a weakness in the black camp. After moving his rook from a1, White may at some point move the c3-knight into the d5-square. Normally Black will not be able to tolerate the knight for too long and will either capture it with the light-squared bishop or force it back with ...e7-e6, the latter possibility leaving Black with a potentially weak d6-pawn.

Black's ideas include ...Nc5, ...Qb6 and ...Rfc8, trying to create some counterplay on the queenside. Often the play will revolve around White trying to push the knight away with a timely b3-b4.

Theoretical?

The Maroczy Bind lines are not very theoretical and can be played very much on general principles. The positions are not sharp and a small mistake is unlikely to meet with severe punishment. The lines without c2-c4, however, are more theoretical (see Game 39) and here it's wise for both players to read up.

Statistics

The Accelerated Dragon has never been quite as popular as the main line Dragon, probably because Black reaches a slightly passive, if somewhat solid, position in the Maroczy Bind variations. I found over 15,000 examples in *Mega Database 2002*, with White scoring 52%. At the highest level (the top 1,000 encounters), White scores 56%. Significantly, though, more than half these games were drawn, underlining the resilience of the Accelerated Dragon.

Illustrative Games

Game 38
□ Vaganian ■ Ivkov
Moscow 1985

1 Nf3 c5 2 c4 g6 3 e4 Bg7 4 d4 cxd4 5 Nxd4 Nc6 6 Be3 Nf6 7 Nc3 d6 8 Be2 0-0 9 0-0 Bd7 10 Qd2 Nxd4 11 Bxd4 Bc6 12 f3 Nd7 13

Be3 a5 14 b3 Nc5

Placing the knight on the useful c5-outpost. It's quite difficult for White to chase this knight away, although this is normally the long-term plan.

15 Rab1

Sensibly removing the rook from the range of the g7-bishop and preparing a2-a3 followed by b3-b4.

15...Qb6 (Diagram 12)

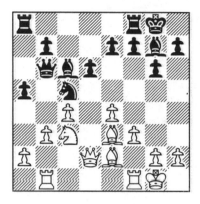

Diagram 12
A manoeuvring game

Diagram 13
White to move and win

Preventing White's plan. Now 16 a3? can be answered by 16...Nxb3! 17 Qd3 Bd4 18 Bxd4 Qxd4+ 19 Qxd4 Nxd4 and Black has won a pawn.

16 Rfc1

Overprotecting the c3-knight as a prophylactic measure against ...Qb4.

16...Rfc8 17 Rc2

Making the final preparations for the queenside expansion. The immediate 17 a3 can still be answered by 17...Nxb3!, for example: 18 Bxb6 Nxd2 19 Rb2 (the knight is trapped but...) 19...Nxc4 20 Bxc4 Bd7! 21 Nd1 Bxb2 22 Nxb2 Rc6 23 Be3 b5 and Black's rook and two pawns are work more than White's two minor pieces in this ending.

After 17 Rc2 White is finally threatening 18 a3, as 18...Nxb3 now fails to 19 Nd1! Nxd2 20 Rxb6, trapping the black knight.

17...Qd8 18 Bf1 Be5

Preparing to create some counterplay with ...e7-e6 and ...Qh4. Now White embarks on an unusual knight manoeuvre.

19 Nd1!?

Planning Nf2-g4, hitting the e5-bishop on the way.

19...Qe8

Now that the knight has moved from c3, Black changes tack and prepares the lunge ...b7-b5.

20 Nf2 b5?!

The prophylactic move 20...Bg7 would have been stronger, preparing to answer 21 Ng4 with 21...h5.

21 Ng4! Bg7 22 cxb5 Bxb5 23 Nh6+

This knight is a thorn in Black's side. Now 23...Kh8 loses a pawn to 24 Nxf7+! Qxf7 25 Bxb5.

23...Kf8 24 Bxb5 Qxb5 25 Qd5

Threatening mate on f7.

25...Qe8 26 e5 Rd8?

26...Ne6 is more resilient.

27 exd6 exd6 28 Re1 Rac8? (Diagram 13)

Again 28...Ne6 gives Black more hope. Now White has a winning tactic.

29 Rxc5! Rxc5

29...dxc5 30 Bxc5+ mates.

30 Qxc5! Black resigns

White wins easily after 30...dxc5 31 Bxc5+ Qe7 32 Bxe7+.

Game 39
□ **Liss** ■ **Sutovsky**
Tel Aviv 1999

---

1 e4 c5 2 Nf3 Nc6 3 Nc3

White adopts an unusual move order, perhaps to avoid the Sveshnikov or the Kalashnikov Variation, but we soon arrive back into an Open Sicilian.

3...g6 4 d4 cxd4 5 Nxd4 Bg7 6 Be3 Nf6 7 Bc4

If White wanted to transpose into a normal Classical Dragon with 7 Be2 he would be in for a bit of a shock. After the further moves 7...0-0 8 0-0, Black need not transpose back into the Dragon with 8...d6. Instead he can play the far more forceful 8...d5!, illustrating one of the advantages of playing the accelerated form of the Dragon. After 9 exd5 Nxd5 10 Nxd5 Qxd5 11 Bf3 Qa5 12 Nxc6 bxc6 13 Bxc6 Rb8 Black is very active.

The sequence 7 f3 0-0 8 Qd2 d5! is another example of the successful ...d7-d5 break; Black is a full tempo up on a normal Yugoslav Attack.

 WARNING: Be very careful when trying to transpose into a favourite line. You may not get what you're after!

7...0-0 8 Bb3

8 f3 Qb6 is annoying for White, as after 9 Bb3 Black can indulge in

favourable complications with 9...Nxe4!.

8...a5

This keeps an Accelerated Dragon flavour to the position. Black prepares ...a5-a4, for example 9 Qd2?! a4! 10 Bxa4 Nxe4! 11 Nxe4 Rxa4 and Black has regained his piece with advantage.

8...d6 is likely to transpose into a main line Yugoslav Attack after 9 f3 Bd7 10 Qd2 Rc8 11 0-0-0 (see Chapter 1).

9 f3

Securing the e4-pawn, but this doesn't prevent Black from creating immense complications.

9...d5!? (Diagram 14)

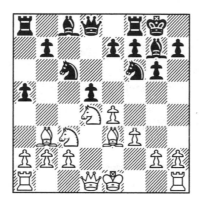

Diagram 14	Diagram 15
Black goes 'all in'	White will 'checkmate' the black queen!

This pawn sacrifice tries to exploit White's lagging development and the slight weakness White's last move created. The resulting lines are extremely theoretical and razor sharp.

10 Bxd5 Nxd5 11 exd5 Nb4

Threatening simply to regain the pawn with ...Nxd5. White must protect the pawn to harbour realistic prospects of keeping an advantage.

12 Nde2 Bf5 13 Rc1 b5 14 a3

After 14 0-0 Black maintains the pressure with 14...Rc8. Liss's choice is more forcing and leads to a long tactical sequence.

14...Nxc2+! 15 Rxc2 Bxc2 16 Qxc2 b4 17 Na4 Qxd5!

Seemingly allowing a material gaining fork.

18 Nb6 Qe6!

Holding Black's position together. Now 19 Nxa8 Qxe3 leaves Black a piece down but with very strong compensation, for example: 20 Nc7 Rc8 (20...Bd4!?) 21 Nd5 Rxc2 22 Nxe3 Rxb2 23 axb4 a4 (this a-pawn is very difficult to stop) 24 Kf2 Bd4! 25 Rd1 (or 25 Ra1 Rxe2+) 25...e5 26 f4 a3 27 fxe5 a2 and Black will follow up with ...Rb1.

19 Kf2 Rab8

The fireworks have finished and the position is roughly level, Black's rook and pawn making up for White's extra two knights.

20 Qc5 Rfd8 21 Re1! Rd6?!

Black should have probably grabbed the pawn with 21...Bxb2.

22 Nf4 Qa2?!

Another mistake. Better is 22...Qf6.

23 Nc8!

White's knight re-enters the game with great effect via the back rank.

23...Rd7 24 Re2 Bf8 25 Nb6 Rdd8 26 a4

Now Black's queen is looking a little silly on a2, but soon it reaches an even worse square!

26...e6 27 Qxa5 Qb1 28 Qe5 Bg7 29 Qc7 Qh1? (Diagram 15) 30 Nxe6! Bf6

Or 30...fxe6 31 Re1! and the black queen is trapped. White uses the same tactic to win the game.

31 Bg5! Bxg5 32 Nxg5 Rf8 33 Re1! Black resigns

The Four Knights Variation

1 e4 c5 2 Nf3 e6 3 d4 cxd4 4 Nxd4 Nf6 5 Nc3 Nc6 (Diagram 16)

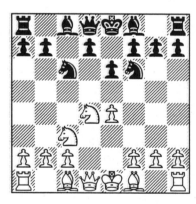

Diagram 16
The Four Knights Variation

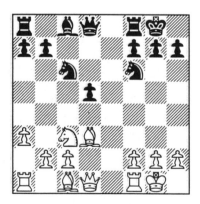

Diagram 17
A typical Four Knights position

There are at least two other systems in the Sicilian where all four knights are developed very quickly (the Classical and the Sveshnikov), but it's this particular variation which is known in chess circles as the Sicilian Four Knights. (Just to confuse matters there are also Four Knights variations in both king's pawn openings and the English Opening.)

The Sicilian Four Knights is another logical looking line for Black, who plans to develop his kingside quickly. Black aims to do without the move ...a7-a6 and White's most critical way to meet the Four Knights is by trying to take advantage of this fact with an early Ndb5.

I should also mention the move 5...Bb4, which is known as the Pin Variation. This line is sharp but not very popular. One possible variation is 6 e5 Nd5 7 Bd2 Nxc3 8 bxc3 Be7 9 Qg4! 0-0 10 Bh6 g6 11 h4! and White has a very quick attack.

6 Ndb5

Threatening Nd6+. White's main alternative is 6 Nxc6 (see Game 41).

6...Bb4

The move 6...d6 is a very important alternative, after which 7 Bf4 e5 8 Bg5 transposes into the main line Sveshnikov. Indeed, in practice the Sveshnikov is sometimes reached in this fashion.

In contrast, 6...d5? 7 exd5 exd5 8 Bf4 is very bad for Black, who has no good way to deal with the threat of Nc7+.

7 a3

The main move. 7 Nd6+ looks attractive on first sight, but 7...Ke7 is actually fine for Black. It's true that he has now lost the right to castle, but following 8 Nxc8+ Rxc8 9 Bd2 d5! Black is well ahead on development and may continue with ...Rhe8 and ...Kf8 to put his king in safety.

Another try for White is 7 Bf4!?, which leads to a very sharp position after 7...Nxe4 8 Qf3 d5 9 0-0-0 Bxc3 10 Nc7+ Kf8 11 bxc3.

7...Bxc3+

Now 7...Ba5? 8 Nd6+ is good for White, as after 8...Ke7 there is no threat to the knight so it can remain on its commanding d6 outpost.

WARNING: Black must not allow White to secure a knight on the d6-square.

8 Nxc3 d5!

Staking a claim for a share of the centre.

9 exd5 exd5 10 Bd3 0-0 11 0-0 (Diagram 17)

Strategies

This is unlike a normal Sicilian position in that Black has space and easy development for his pieces. On the other hand, it's White who has the better pawn structure; Black's isolated pawn on d5 may prove to be a weakness in the long run. White may also hope to exploit his bishop pair in a position which is quite open.

Theoretical?

The main line reaching Diagram 17 is not theoretical at all, but those wishing to play the 7 Bf4 variation with either colour are well advised to learn their stuff!

Statistics

The main line with 6...Bb4 has never been very popular as most Sicilian players are not looking to reach the type of position seen in Diagram 17. I found just over 1,700 games with 6...Bb4 in *Mega Database 2002*, with White scoring well with 60%.

Illustrative Games

Game 40
□ **Shmuter** ■ **Khmelnitsky**
Lvov 1990

1 e4 c5 2 Nf3 e6 3 d4 cxd4 4 Nxd4 Nf6 5 Nc3 Nc6 6 Ndb5 Bb4 7 a3 Bxc3+ 8 Nxc3 d5 9 exd5 exd5 10 Bd3 0-0 11 0-0 d4

Black advances his isolated pawn and puts the question to the knight on c3.

12 Ne2 Bg4

Another sensible move, developing a piece and pinning the white knight to the queen.

13 Bg5

The move 13 f3, breaking the pin, is also possible but White prefers to utilise another pin, this time on the f6-knight.

13...h6

A simpler way to unpin would be with 13...Qd6.

14 Bh4 g5? (Diagram 18)

It's not worth weakening the kingside in this manner just to break the pin. This decision will come back to haunt Black later on.

TIP: Think long and hard before ever weakening your king's position.

15 Bg3 Qd5 16 f3 Bh5 17 c4!

Inducing an opening of the position. Black gets rid of his isolated pawn but White's bishops begin to show their influence on the game.

NOTE: Bishops like open positions.

17...dxc3 18 Nxc3 Qd4+ 19 Bf2 Qd7 20 Ne4 Qe6 21 Nc5 Qe5 22 Nxb7 Rab8

Or 22...Qxb2 23 Rb1 Qe5 (23...Qxa3 24 Bc5) 24 Re1 Qc7 25 Bg3 Qc8 26 Nd6 (Shmuter) and the knight will arrive with great effect on f5.

23 Nd6! (Diagram 19)

The knight cannot be captured due to Bh7+.

23...Rfd8 24 Nc4 Qf4 25 Kh1!

White is a pawn up and Black's position is still riddled with weaknesses. The rest is quite straightforward.

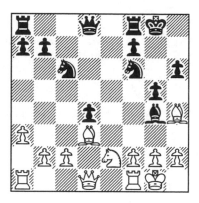

Diagram 18
Black weakens his kingside

Diagram 19
White uses tactics to save his knight

25...Bg6 26 Bg3 Qd4

Or 26...Rxd3 27 Bxf4 Rxd1 28 Rfxd1 gxf4 29 Rd6 and White wins one of the knights.

27 Bxg6 Qxc4 28 Qc1! Black resigns

Resignation is perhaps a little early. Black can play on, although 28...Qxc1 29 Raxc1 fxg6 30 Rxc6 is not much fun.

Game 41
□ **Yudasin** ■ **Kramnik**
Wijk aan Zee (5th matchgame) 1994

---

1 e4 c5 2 Nf3 Nc6 3 d4 cxd4 4 Nxd4 Nf6 5 Nc3 e6 6 Nxc6 bxc6 7 e5

The logical follow-up to White's last move. The black knight is forced to move from f6.

7...Nd5 8 Ne4

Again the best move. White plans to harass the black knight with a timely c2-c4.

8 Nxd5?! cxd5 would only serve to strengthen Black's centre. Black would follow up with a swift ...d7-d6.

8...Qc7

Black must react positively so that White cannot simply carry out the idea of c2-c4. First the e5-pawn is targeted.

9 f4 Qa5+

Now that White has slightly weakened himself with f2-f4, Black tries to create further counterplay. The immediate 9...Qb6 is the main alternative.

10 Bd2!?

After this move White must be willing to sacrifice a pawn. Safer is 10 c3.

10...Qb6

The third move in a row, but the queen has now settled on a good post, where it prevents White from castling kingside and also hits the b2-pawn.

11 Bd3!

Offering a pawn. 11 c4 Qd4! would exploit the slight disharmony in the white camp.

11...Be7

Black does well to decline the offer. After 11...Qxb2 12 0-0! White solves his castling problem and his development advantage is beginning to assume greater significance.

12 Rb1?

Simply protecting the b-pawn is too passive. White should play 12 Qe2, again with good play for the pawn after 12...Qxb2 13 0-0.

12...Ba6 13 Qe2 Bxd3 14 Qxd3 f5! (Diagram 20)

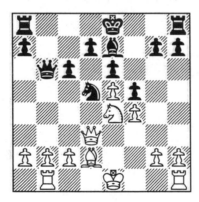 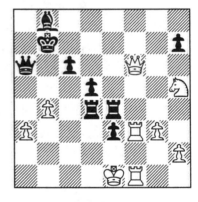

Diagram 20
Black forces a decision

Diagram 21
The white king is under fire

Forcing White to either exchange on f6 or remove his knight from the excellent e4-square.

15 exf6 gxf6!? 16 f5 0-0-0

White has some problems in this position as he cannot castle on either side.

17 a3 Rhe8 18 Kf1 exf5 19 Ng3 f4 20 Nf5 Bf8 21 b4 Ne3+?

This allows White right back into the game. In his notes in *Informator* Kramnik suggests the line 21...Re5, answering 22 c4 with 22...Rde8!. For example: 23 cxd5 Rxd5 24 Qc2 Qb5+ 25 Kg1 Rxf5 and

Black is two pawns ahead.

22 Bxe3 fxe3 23 Ke2 d5 24 Rhf1

Black is a pawn up, but it's difficult to get at the white king, which is well shielded by the pawn on e3.

24...Re4 25 c3 Bd6 26 Rf3 Bb8 27 g3 Rde8 28 Rbf1 a5!

The best way to achieve play is by striking on the queenside. White's position is still solid, but in the next few moves Yudasin begins to drift badly.

29 Ng7?! R8e7 30 Nh5?

White should offer a repetition with 30 Nf5.

30...axb4 31 cxb4? Rd4!

Now Black's attack is fully back on the rails.

32 Qf5+ Kb7 33 Qxf6 Qa6+ 34 Ke1 Ree4 (Diagram 21)

Threatening the devastating ...Qd3.

35 Qg7+ Ka8 36 Rf8 Rd1+! 37 Kxd1 e2+ White resigns

38 Kd2 exf1Q is easily winning for Black.

The Kan Variation

1 e4 c5 2 Nf3 e6 3 d4 cxd4 4 Nxd4 a6 (Diagram 22)

Diagram 22
The Kan Variation

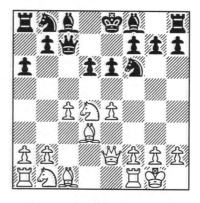

Diagram 23
A typical Kan position

Most players now name this opening after the Russian International Master Ilya Kan, but it's also been attributed to Louis Paulsen, one of the great theoreticians of the 19th century. The great advantage of the Kan Variation is its flexibility. Black waits with pawn moves and doesn't commit any of his pieces until White has shown his hand. On the other hand, Black must be careful not to fall too far behind in development, while the lack of any real pressure on White's centre allows White to set up a Maroczy Bind with an early c2-c4.

5 Bd3

The main move for White, who develops a piece and gets ready to castle. With 5 Bd3 White keeps the option open of going c2-c4. For 5 Nc3 see Game 43, while White can also set up an immediate bind with 5 c4.

5...Nf6

Finally a black piece comes out!

6 0-0

6 e5? loses a pawn to 6...Qa5+ but now e4-e5 is a threat, which Black's next move prevents.

6...Qc7 7 Qe2

Once again White introduces the possibility of e4-e5.

7...d6

Finally putting a stop to any e4-e5 ideas, at least for the moment. Now Black has settled on a Scheveningen structure. If White were to play 8 Nc3 then play would very much resemble a 'Schevy', but most players opt to construct the Maroczy Bind.

8 c4 (Diagram 23)

Strategies

White's undoubted space advantage presents him with many different options of attack, although he usually develops normally and waits for Black to commit himself before choosing a plan. One option is a typical Sicilian thrust with f2-f4, creating ideas of either f4-f5 or e4-e5. Another, more solid, idea is to play f2-f3, resisting play on the kingside and favouring an attack on the other side of the board, while always being on the lookout to prevent Black freeing himself with ...d6-d5.

Black is slightly passive but his 'hedgehog' structure is very resilient and counterplay is always lurking: possible ...d6-d5 or ...b6-b5 pawn breaks nibbling away at the white centre. In general, however, play is often slow moving.

 NOTE: It requires some patience to play the Kan Variation.

Theoretical?

These lines with c2-c4 are generally less theoretical than those where White omits c2-c4 in favour of Nc3. The reason is that White is going for a long-term advantage rather than a quick kill, so the lines are generally not so sharp and are more positionally based.

Statistics

At international level the Kan's flexibility has enticed many followers, especially in the last decade. Many of today's top players have used the Kan, although this tends to be more as a secondary weapon rather than their main choice. I found over 19,000 games in *Mega Database 2002*, with White scoring 50%, although black players were slightly higher rated on average.

Illustrative Games

Game 42
□ **Hracek** ■ **Urday**
Yerevan Olympiad 1996

1 e4 c5 2 Nf3 e6 3 d4 cxd4 4 Nxd4 a6 5 Bd3 Nf6 6 0-0 Qc7 7 Qe2 d6 8 c4 g6

This fianchetto has become popular in recent years. Black figures that a bishop on g7 will protect his king well against any kingside action from White. Classical development with 8...Be7 is the main alternative.

9 Nc3 Bg7 10 Rd1

Now that Black has committed himself, White begins a very straightforward plan of hitting the slightly vulnerable d6-pawn. This entails shifting some pieces off the d-file.

10...0-0 11 Nf3 Nbd7 12 Bf4 (Diagram 24)

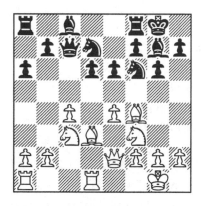
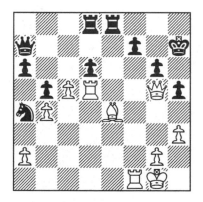

Diagram 24	Diagram 25
White targets the d6-pawn	White's attack crashes through

Adding further pressure to d6. To relieve the pressure, Black decides to annoy the bishop with his knight.

12...Nh5

12...Ng4, followed by ...Nge5, is another idea.

13 Bg5 h6 14 Be3 Re8

Preparing to defend the d-pawn in certain lines with ...Bf8.

15 Rac1 b6

Black completes his hedgehog formation and prepares to fianchetto with ...Bb7.

16 Qd2 Kh7 17 Bb1 Bf8 18 h3!

An imaginative idea. White plans to pressure the h6-pawn with Nh2-g4.

18...Bb7 19 Nh2 Nhf6 20 b3 Rad8 21 Ng4 Ng8

Black is still relatively solid, but his lack of real counterplay gives White a comfortable edge.

22 Bd4! h5 23 Nh2 Ngf6 24 Nf3 Kg8 25 Ng5 Qb8 26 f4!

After some slow manoeuvring, White steps up a gear and pushes on the kingside.

26...Nh7?!

26...Bg7 is more resilient, according to Hracek.

27 Nxh7 Kxh7 28 Rf1 Bh6 29 Be3 Bc6 30 Rcd1!

Again the d-pawn becomes a target.

30...Nc5 31 b4 Na4 32 f5!

Excellent play by Hracek, who is combining pressure on the d-file with an attack against the black king.

32...Bxe3+ 33 Qxe3 exf5 34 Nd5?

Even stronger is Hracek's suggestion of 34 Nxa4! Bxa4 35 Qg5!, for example: 35...Bxd1 36 exf5! Rd7 37 fxg6+ fxg6 38 Bxg6+ Kh8 39 Bxe8 Qxe8 40 Rxd1 and White has a winning advantage.

34...Bxd5 35 Rxd5 b5!

The only chance of counterplay.

36 Qg5! Qa7+ 37 c5 fxe4?

37...Qe7! keeps Black in the game.

38 Bxe4! (Diagram 25) 38...Qe7

Black has no good defence. 38...Nc3 39 Rdf5! is winning for White, for example: 39...Rf8 40 Rxf7+ Rxf7 41 Qxg6+ Kh8 42 Rxf7.

39 Rf6 Qxe4 40 Rxf7+ Kg8 41 Qf6 Black resigns

After 41...Qe3+ 42 Kh2 Qh6 43 Rg5 Black's position collapses.

Game 43
□ **Shirov** ■ **Svidler**
Tilburg 1997

---

1 e4 c5 2 Nf3 e6 3 d4 cxd4 4 Nxd4 a6 5 Nc3

With this move White indicates that he is quite happy to develop classically as a precursor to a usual kingside attack.

5...b5 6 Bd3 Qb6

This is a reasonably modern idea. Black wants to kick the white knight away from the centre before settling on c7, the normal square for the queen.

7 Nb3 Qc7 8 f4 d6 9 Qf3 Nd7

Finally Black begins to develop some pieces around his carefully constructed pawn structure.

10 0-0 Ngf6 11 Bd2 b4!?

Black could also continue with 11...Bb7 or 11...Be7.

12 Nd1 Bb7 13 Nf2

13 Bxb4?? drops a piece to the fork 13...Qb6+.

TIP: Always be aware of tactics involving the g1-a7 diagonal and White's king on g1.

13...a5 (Diagram 26)

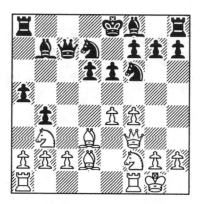

Diagram 26
White should attack on the kingside

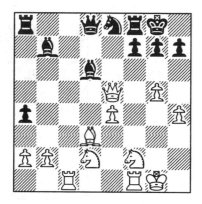

Diagram 27
Black rules the dark squares

14 c3?!

Svidler preferred the more aggressive 14 g4!?, planning to kick the black knight with g4-g5.

14...bxc3 15 Bxc3 Be7 16 Rac1 Qb6! 17 g4?!

As I said before, this move should have been played earlier. Black is now in much better shape to combat the idea.

17...a4 18 Bd4 Qd8 19 Nd2 0-0 20 g5 Ne8 21 h4 e5!

Black suddenly breaks out.

22 Bc3 exf4 23 Qxf4 Ne5! 24 Bxe5

The winning of this pawn was clearly very risky, but Black was already threatening to open the position with ...f7-f6.

24...dxe5 25 Qxe5 Bd6 (Diagram 27)

As so often in the Open Sicilian, a pawn is a small price to pay for complete control over the dark squares. Even so, it's surprising how quickly White's position collapses.

26 Qf5 g6 27 Qf3 Be5 28 Nc4 Bd4 29 Rcd1 f5!

Opening up the position with 30 gxf6 Nxf6 would be suicide, e.g. 31 Qe2 Qc7 32 e5 Qc6! and White will be mated along the long diagonal. Still, the move chosen also does little to halt Black's progress.

30 Be2 fxe4 31 Qg3 Ng7! 32 Qd6 Nf5 33 Qe6+ Kh8 34 Nd6 Qc7! 35 Nxf5 Rxf5 White resigns

36 Rxd4 allows 36...Qg3+ 37 Kh1 e3+ 38 Ne4 Qxh4+ 39 Kg2 Rxg5+ 40 Kf3 Qg3 mate, while 36 Kg2 runs into a nasty discovered check with ...e4-e3. A convincing game by Svidler.

The Kalashnikov Variation

1 e4 c5 2 Nf3 Nc6 3 d4 cxd4 4 Nxd4 e5 (Diagram 28)

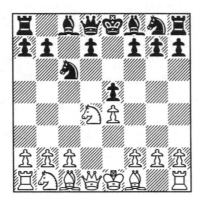
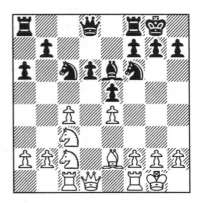

Diagram 28	Diagram 29
The Kalashnikov Variation	A typical Kalashnikov position

Black makes an immediate attack on the d4-knight, forcing it to leave its central post. The Kalashnikov is a very close relation to the Sveshnikov and sometimes it simply transposes.

5 Nb5

Once again the knight must move to this threatening square if White is looking for an advantage. Both 5 Nf3 Nf6 6 Nc3 Bb4 and 5 Nf5 Nf6 6 Nc3 d5 are fine for Black, as we saw in the Sveshnikov.

5...d6

Preventing Nd6+. The sequence 5...a6 6 Nd6+ Bxd6 7 Qxd6 Qf6 is known as the Löwenthal Variation and is played from time to time. White can either exchange queens or play 8 Qd1, 8 Qa3 or 8 Qc7!?.

6 c4

Once again creating the Maroczy Bind and thus putting a stop to any ...d6-d5 ideas.

The main alternative is 6 N1c3 and now after 6...a6 7 Na3 b5 8 Nd5 Nf6 9 Bg5 we have transposed to the 9 Nd5 variation of the Sveshnikov. If Black wants to keep an independent flavour he can try

8...Nge7 or 8...Nce7!?.

6...Be7!

There is a point of developing this bishop ahead of the g8-knight which will become apparent in a couple of moves.

7 N1c3 a6 8 Na3

As with the Sveshnikov, this knight is forced back to the miserable a3-square, but this time it will be easy to relocate it via c2.

8...Be6 9 Be2 Bg5!

The point of Black's previous play. With this move he prepares to trade his 'bad bishop' for White's 'good bishop', which is positionally very desirable.

10 Nc2

Covering d4, which could become an outpost for Black's c6-knight.

The pawn grab 10 Bxg5 Qxg5 11 Qxd6?? leads to disaster after 11...Rd8 12 Qc5 Qd2+ 13 Kf1 Qxb2 and White can already resign.

TIP: Look long and hard before you grab a pawn.

10...Bxc1 11 Rxc1 Nf6 12 0-0 0-0 (Diagram 29)

Strategies

White can try to exert pressure on the d6-pawn with Qd2 and Rfd1, but this is usually countered by ...Qb8! and ...Rfd8. The black queen can then emerge via the a7-square, where it controls the long a7-g1 diagonal. Black will sometimes look to break with ...b7-b5, while both players must be on the lookout for possible Nd5 for White and ...Nd4 for Black.

Theoretical?

Not really. Play is quiet and of a positional nature. Plans are much more important here than any individual moves.

Statistics

The Kalashnikov is a very modern opening and so there is considerably less practical experience with it. I found just over 4,000 games in *Mega Database 2002*, with White scoring 52%.

Illustrative Games

Game 44
□ **Asrian** ■ **Sveshnikov**
St Petersburg 1997

1 e4 c5 2 Nf3 Nc6 3 d4 cxd4 4 Nxd4 e5 5 Nb5 d6 6 c4 Be7 7 N1c3 a6 8 Na3 Be6 9 Be2 Bg5 10 0-0 Bxc1 11 Rxc1 Nf6 12 Nc2 0-0 13

Qd2

Preparing to pressurise d6 with Rfd1.

13...Qb8!

A good response, vacating the d8-square for the rook and preparing to play ...Qa7.

14 Qe3

White takes the diagonal first, so this merely leads to a queen exchange.

14...Qa7 15 Qxa7 Nxa7 16 Rfd1 Rfd8 17 f3

Supporting the e4-pawn and thus freeing the c3-knight of this duty.

17...Rac8 18 b3 Kf8

Activating the king, always a useful thing to do in endgames.

The advance 18...b5 is also possible, as 19 cxb5? loses material after 19...Rxc3.

19 Nb4 Nc6 (Diagram 30)

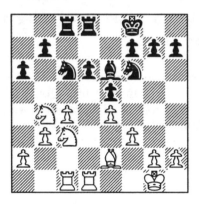

Diagram 30
Both sides are content with a draw

20 Nxc6

After this move the game soon ends in a draw as the players repeat moves.

The line 20 Nbd5 Bxd5 21 Nxd5 Nxd5 22 cxd5 Nd4! is an illustration of how a few careless exchanges can affect the game. The knight has a good outpost on d4 and is clearly superior to the white bishop.

20...Rxc6 21 Nd5 Rdc8 22 Nb4 Rb6 23 Nd5 Rbc6 24 Nb4 Rb6 25 Nd5 Draw agreed

Summary

1) The Taimanov is a flexible variation which is gaining popularity at the highest levels.

2) The Accelerated Dragon is certainly more resolute than the mainline Dragon, but Black must be careful not to drift into a passive position against the dreaded Maroczy Bind.

3) The Kan is yet another flexible line, which leads to many different possibilities for both sides.

4) The Kalashnikov is a modern opening that often leads to relatively blocked positions. Black's structure is extremely difficult to break down.

5) The Four Knights Variation leads to some unusual positions for the Sicilian, but Black must be prepared to take on an isolated pawn.

Chapter Seven

Bb5 Systems

-  The Rossolimo Variation
- The Moscow Variation

The Rossolimo Variation

1 e4 c5 2 Nf3 Nc6 3 Bb5 (Diagram 1)

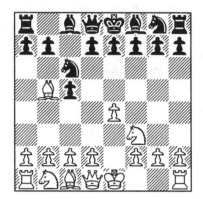

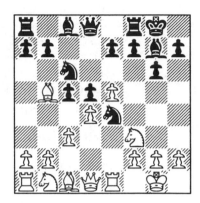

Diagram 1
The Rossolimo Variation

Diagram 2
A typical Rossolimo position

This line, named after the Russian Grandmaster Nicolas Rossolimo, is an important alternative to the Open Sicilian. White develops a piece, puts pressure along the a4-e8 diagonal, prepares to castle and leaves central issues very much open.

3...g6

Preparing to fianchetto the king's bishop is Black's most popular response. For the main alternative, 3...e6, see Game 47.

4 0-0

A logical choice. White castles before deciding on a course of action. That said, the immediate exchange with 4 Bxc6 has been growing in popularity (see Game 46).

4...Bg7 5 Re1

Supporting the e4-pawn. The sequence 5 c3 Nf6 6 Re1 will transpose into the text, although White can also try 6 e5 Nd5 7 d4 cxd4 8 cxd4.

5...Nf6

5...e5, preparing ...Nge7, is also possible. White usually captures with 6 Bxc6, after which Black can choose to capture with either pawn.

6 c3!

A crucial move. White wishes to play d2-d4, but after ...cxd4 White intends recapturing with the c-pawn, thus keeping two pawns in the centre. This strategy very much differs from that in Open Sicilians.

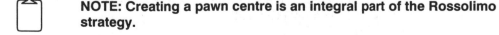

NOTE: Creating a pawn centre is an integral part of the Rossolimo strategy.

6...0-0 7 d4 d5!

It's paramount that Black strikes back in the centre, otherwise he could risk ending up in a passive position. Black can, however, exchange on d4 first and only then play ...d7-d5.

8 e5

Gaining space in the centre. 8 exd5 Qxd5 9 Bxc6 Qxc6 10 Rxe7 leaves White a pawn up, but after 10...Be6! White will find it virtually impossible to extract his rook. One grim example from White's point of view was 11 Ne5 Qc8 (threatening ...Nd5) 12 c4 cxd4 13 Bg5 Ne4 14 Bf4 Bxe5! 15 Bxe5 Qc5 16 Qxd4 Rad8! and White resigned in Antunes-Neverov, Candas 1992.

8...Ne4 (Diagram 2)

Strategies

White has more space in the centre but Black's pieces (especially the knight on e4) are very well placed. White will try to maintain his pawn centre and either exchange off or, in rare cases, try to trap the knight on e4. Black will sometimes try to destroy White's centre with a timely ...f7-f6.

Theoretical?

Not really. There are quite a few different options for both sides, but no real critical continuations where one slip could mean disaster.

Statistics

The Rossolimo looks to be an ideal choice for those wishing to avoid the theoretical Open Sicilians after 2...Nc6. In *Mega Database 2002* there were over 15,000 examples of the Rossolimo, with White scoring a healthy 57%. Its highest rated advocate is Garry Kasparov, although he has generally reserved it for rapidplay games and simultaneous displays.

Illustrative Games

Game 45
□ **Ardeleanu** ■ **Grigore**
Iasi 1999

1 e4 c5 2 Nf3 Nc6 3 Bb5 g6 4 0-0 Bg7 5 c3 Nf6 6 Re1 0-0 7 d4 d5 8 e5 Ne4 9 Bxc6

Also possible is the immediate 9 Nbd2.

9...bxc6 10 Nbd2 cxd4 11 cxd4 Bf5

Black tries to keep a piece on the e4-square. The main alternatives here are 11...c5 and 11...Nxd2

12 Nf1 f6!

Black must do something positive or else White will play Nh4 and then trap the knight with f2-f3.

13 exf6 exf6 14 Ng3 Nxg3 15 hxg3 Qb6

Black's pawn structure has been slightly weakened but he has the long-term potential of the two bishops. Overall, this leads to a dynamic equality.

16 b3 Rfe8 17 Ba3?!

White should avoid giving Black the chance to activate his dark-squared bishop as he does on the next move.

17...Bh6!

This move is annoying for White, who cannot now use the c1-square for a rook.

18 Be7 Kf7 19 Bc5 Qa6 (Diagram 3)

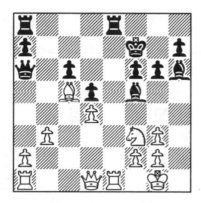

Diagram 3
Black's bishops rake across the board

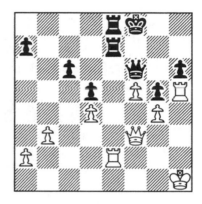

Diagram 4
White's rook is caught offside

20 g4?!

Dissatisfied with normal continuations, White sacrifices a pawn to complicate.

20...Bxg4 21 Ne5+ fxe5 22 Qxg4 e4 23 Qh4 Bg7! 24 Re3

Exercise 7: How does Black react to 24 Qxh7 here?

24...Kg8 25 Rh3 h6 26 Qg4 g5 27 f4 Qc8!

The queen comes back to defend just in time. Now Black is simply a clear pawn up.

28 f5 Rf8 29 Rf1 Rf7 30 Rh5 Qd8 31 Qh3 Qf6 32 Kh1 Re8 33 g4 e3!

TIP: Passed pawns must be pushed!

34 Re1 e2 35 Qf3 Bf8! 36 Bxf8 Kxf8 37 Rxe2 Rfe7 (Diagram 4)

White has regained the pawn but now his rook on h5 is right out of play. He pays the ultimate penalty for this.

38 Rxe7 Qxe7 39 Kg2 Qe1! 40 Rxh6 Re2+ 41 Kh3 Re3

Pinning and winning the queen.

42 Rf6+ Kg7 White resigns

Game 46
☐ **Oral** ■ **P.Jelen**
Trencin 1995

1 e4 c5 2 Nf3 Nc6 3 Bb5 g6 4 Bxc6 dxc6

4...bxc6 is also very playable. In that case White should simply castle and prepare action in the centre with Re1, c2-c3 and d2-d4.

5 h3 Bg7 6 d3!?

With the d-file half-open, Black is much better prepared to meet d2-d4 so White adopts a different approach.

6...Nf6 7 Nc3 0-0 8 Be3!

Now we see one of the advantages of capturing on c6 on move four rather than castling. In this position White can play in 'Yugoslav Attack' fashion with Qd2, Bh6 and queenside castling.

8...b6 9 Qd2 (Diagram 5)

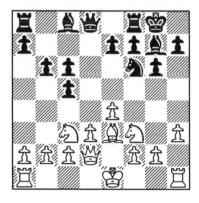

Diagram 5	Diagram 6
White prepares queenside castling	White uses interference

9...Re8

Supporting the ...e7-e5 advance and planning to meet Bh6 with ...Bh8.

10 Bh6 Bh8 11 e5!? Nd5 12 Ne4 Bf5 13 0-0-0 a5 14 g4 Be6

14...Bxe4? 15 dxe4 Nb4 16 Qf4! Qc7 17 a3 Na6 18 h4 and White's attack is far quicker than Black's.

15 Rdg1 Qc7 16 h4 Red8

Black can grab a pawn with 16...Bxe5 but after 17 Nxe5 Qxe5 18 f4 Qc7 19 f5 Bd7 20 h5 he will find it difficult to survive the onslaught.

17 h5 a4 18 hxg6 fxg6 19 Neg5 a3 20 b3

Naturally White tries to keep the queenside as closed as possible.

20...Bc8 21 Re1!?

Now things become extremely complicated.

21...Bxg4 22 Nxh7! Bxf3

But not 22...Kxh7? 23 Bf8+! Bh5 (or 23...Kg8 24 Rxh8+ Kxh8 25 Qh6+ Kg8 26 Qg7 mate) 24 Rxh5+ gxh5 25 Qh6+ Kg8 26 Rg1+ Kf7 27 Qg6+ Kxf8 28 Qg8 mate.

23 Qg5

Threatening a decisive capture on g6.

23...Rd6!

An ingenious defence. Now 24 exd6 Bb2+ 25 Kd2 (25 Kb1?? allows a nice mate with 25...Nc3) 25...Bc3+ 26 Kc1 and Black has at least a draw by perpetual check.

24 Rh3!? Re6!

24...Kxh7 still loses after 25 Bf8+! Bh5 26 Rxh5+ gxh5 27 Qf5+ Rg6 28 Rg1 Nf4 29 Rxg6 Nxg6 30 Qf7+ Bg7 31 Qxg7 mate.

25 Rxf3 Bxe5? (Diagram 6)

Finally Black crumbles under pressure. After the calm 25...Kxh7! I can't find anything for White.

26 Nf6+!!

Using the theme of interference, White makes sure that the g6-pawn falls and so does Black's position.

26...Rxf6 27 Rxf6 exf6 28 Qxg6+ Kh8 29 Rh1 Bb2+ 30 Kd2 Bc3+ 31 Kd1 Black resigns

Mate along the h-file cannot be prevented (31...Qh7 is answered by 32 Bg7+!).

Game 47
□ **Wahls** ■ **Rajkovic**
German Bundesliga 1992

1 e4 c5 2 Nf3 Nc6 3 Bb5 e6

A different approach. Black plans ...Nge7 in order to give the knight on c6 more support.

4 0-0 Nge7 5 c3

Once again White plans on building a solid centre with d2-d4, recapturing on d4 with the c3-pawn. Another idea is the preparatory 5 Re1.

5...a6 6 Ba4 d5?!

It looks logical to push in the centre, but Black should probably proceed more carefully with 6...b5, for example: 7 Bc2 Bb7 8 d4 cxd4 9 cxd4 Nb4!, exchanging off White's bishop.

7 exd5 Qxd5 8 d4 b5? (Diagram 7)

This move meets with a stunning refutation. Black should be content either to capture on d4 or play 8...Bd7.

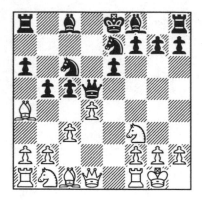

Diagram 7	Diagram 8
Where does the bishop go? Nowhere!	There are too many pins

9 c4!! Qd6

The main point is that 9...Qxc4 loses the queen in mid-board after 10 Bb3 Qb4 11 Bd2. The move 9...bxc4 is also quite unappealing after 10 Nc3 Qd6 11 Ne5 Bb7 12 Ne4.

10 cxb5 Nxd4 11 bxa6+ Nec6?

Now Black is in big trouble. 11...Bd7 would have certainly limited the damage.

12 Bf4! Qd5

Or 12...Qxf4 13 Nxd4 and Black can already resign with a clear conscience.

13 Nxd4 cxd4 14 Nc3! (Diagram 8) Black resigns

It's all over after 14...dxc3 15 Qxd5 exd5 16 Bxc6+ or 14...Qd7 15 Nb5 (threatening Nc7+) 15...e5 16 Bxe5! Nxe5 17 Nc7+.

The Moscow Variation

1 e4 c5 2 Nf3 d6 3 Bb5+ (Diagram 9)

The Moscow Variation has many similarities to the Rossolimo. If anything, the types of positions reached are generally even quieter.

3...Bd7

3...Nc6 is an important alternative and can also be reached via the move order 2 Nf3 Nc6 3 Bb5. See Game 49 for this move.

3...Nd7!? is certainly playable but is rather risky as Black may fall behind on development. A sample line runs 4 d4 Ngf6 5 Nc3 a6 6 Bxd7+ Nxd7 7 0-0 e6 8 Bg5 Qc7.

4 Bxd7+ Qxd7

The normal recapture. Black plans to put his b8-knight on the more active c6-square.

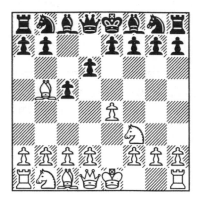

Diagram 9	Diagram 10
The Moscow Variation	A typical Moscow position

5 c4

Aiming for a Maroczy Bind after d2-d4. The main alternative is to build a classical pawn centre with c2-c3 and d2-d4. An adventurous line is 5 0-0 Nc6 6 c3 Nf6 7 d4!? (7 Re1 e6 8 d4 cxd4 9 cxd4 d5 looks equal) 7...Nxe4 8 d5 Ne5 9 Re1 Nxf3+ 10 Qxf3 Nf6 11 c4 with some pressure for the pawn.

5...Nc6 6 0-0 Nf6

The immediate 6...g6 leads to similar play after 7 d4 cxd4 8 Nxd4 Bg7 9 Be3 Nf6 10 f3 0-0 11 Nc3.

7 Nc3 g6

The move 7...e5 prevents d2-d4, but is not popular as it leaves Black with a rather passive bishop on f8, blocked in by its own pawns.

TIP: Look after your pieces!

8 d4 cxd4 9 Nxd4 Bg7 10 Nde2 (Diagram 10)

10 Be3 Ng4 is rather annoying for White, while 10 f3? Nxe4! wins a pawn in a typical Dragon way.

Strategies

Play is very similar to the Maroczy Bind in the Accelerated Dragon. The general feeling is, however, that the exchange of one set of minor pieces has slightly eased Black's task, as he has less chance of ending up in a cramped position. Play is generally slow with both players manoeuvring their pieces to their optimum posts. Both sides must be aware of opportunities for Black to break out with ...d7-d5 (supported by ...e7-e6) and ...b7-b5 (supported by ...a7-a6).

Theoretical?

Certainly not. Play is of a quiet and positional nature, while plans and piece deployment are much more important than any particular moves.

Statistics

According to *Mega Database 2002*, The Moscow Variation is not quite as popular, nor as successful, as the Rossolimo. There were over 10,000 examples, with White scoring 51%. Also, the draw was the most likely result, occurring in 40% of the games.

Illustrative Games

Game 48
☐ **Damljanovic** ■ **Stohl**
Batumi 1999

1 e4 c5 2 Nf3 d6 3 Bb5+ Bd7 4 Bxd7+ Qxd7 5 c4 Nc6 6 0-0 Nf6 7 Nc3 g6 8 d4 cxd4 9 Nxd4 Bg7 10 Nde2 Qe6!?

An interesting counter-attack on the c4- and e4-pawns, which was introduced in the famous Kasparov versus the World Internet match in 1999.

The more solid option is 10...0-0, for example: 11 f3 a6 12 a4 Qd8!? (the queen wants to come to b6 or a5) 13 Be3 Qa5 14 Rc1 Nd7 15 b3 Nc5 with an equal position, Kramnik-Gelfand, Sanghi Nagar (7th matchgame) 1994.

11 Qb3

The critical move must be Kasparov's choice of 11 Nd5 Qxe4 12 Nc7+ Kd7 13 Nxa8 Qxc4 14 Nb6+ axb6 15 Nc3 Ra8, although Black's two extra pawns do provide good compensation for the exchange.

11...0-0

11...Nxe4?? 12 Qxb7 wins a piece with a double attack.

12 Nf4 Qc8 13 Nfd5 e6 (Diagram 11)

Black's d6-pawn may become weak later on, but Stohl decides that this is a small price to pay for ejecting the white knight from d5.

14 Nxf6+ Bxf6 15 Bh6 Rd8 16 Rac1 Ne5 17 Ne2?

After this move White becomes very passively placed. Slovakian GM Lubomir Ftacnik suggests the improvement 17 Qd1! Qc6 (17...Qxc4? 18 Nd5 and 17...Nxc4? 18 b3 Nb6 19 Nd5 are good for White) 18 b3 a6, with an equal position.

17...Qc6 18 Qc2 Rac8 19 b3 d5!

With this move Stohl eliminates his one weakness and assumes the initiative.

20 exd5 exd5 21 Nd4 Qd7 22 c5 Ng4 23 Be3

The only move to avoid losing a piece.

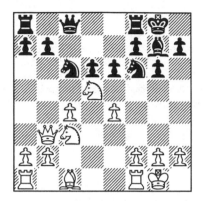

Diagram 11
Black puts the question to the d5-knight

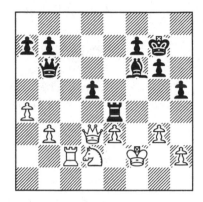

Diagram 12
Black has a winning tactic

23...Re8 24 Qd3

Or 24 Rfe1 Nxe3 25 fxe3 Rxe3! 26 Rxe3 Bxd4 27 Qd2 Bxc5 and Black will emerge two pawns ahead.

24...Nxe3 25 fxe3

Now it is White who has the major weakness: the isolated pawn on e3.

25...Bg5 26 Rfe1 Qe7

Hitting both c5 and e3. One pawn must drop.

27 Kf2 Rxc5 28 Rxc5 Qxc5 29 Nf3 Bf6 30 Re2 Kg7 31 g3 h5 32 Rc2 Qb6 33 a4?

A mistake in time trouble. Now the b3-pawn is also weak. Black immediate exploits this factor.

33...Re4

The rook is coming to b4.

34 Nd2 (Diagram 12)

Allowing a simple combination.

34...Rxe3! 35 Qb5

35 Qxe3 Bd4 pins and wins the queen.

35...Rxb3+ White resigns

36 Qxb6 Rxb6 leaves Black three pawns up in the endgame.

Game 49
□ **Morozevich** ■ **Petursson**
London 1994

---

1 e4 c5 2 Nf3 Nc6 3 Bb5 d6

Black develops his queenside first and plans to unpin the knight with ...Bd7. Of course this position can also be reached via 2...d6 3 Bb5+ Nc6.

4 0-0 Bd7 5 Re1

White can also play 5 c3, but first he plays this preparatory move, allowing the bishop to retreat to f1 after being attacked by ...a7-a6.

5...Nf6

5...a6 should be met by either 6 Bf1 or 6 Bxc6, but certainly not 6 Ba4?? b5 7 Bb3 c4 and the bishop has had a short life!

6 c3 a6 7 Bf1

7 Ba4 is also very playable.

7...Bg4

The bishop has finished its job on d7 and now exerts indirect pressure on the white centre by pinning the f3-knight.

8 d4 cxd4 9 cxd4 d5

Black strikes back in the centre. The other way to do this was with 9...e5!?.

10 e5 Ng8

10...Ne4 doesn't look bad either.

11 Be3 e6 12 a3! (Diagram 13)

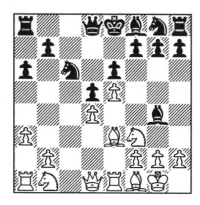

Diagram 13
White has a space advantage

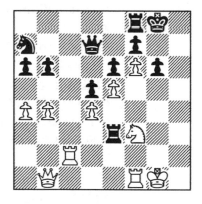

Diagram 14
How can White win at once?

A good move, preventing any black piece from coming to b4. The sequence 12 Nbd2 Bb4! puts both of White's knights in annoying pins.

12...Nge7 13 Nbd2 Nf5 14 Bd3 Be7 15 Qb1 Qd7 16 b4 Bh5 17 Ra2 0-0 18 h3 Kh8 19 Rf1 Rac8 20 g4 Nxe3 21 fxe3 Bg6 22 Bxg6 hxg6 23 Nb3 Na7?

Morozevich preferred the move 23...b6!, keeping White's knight out of c5.

24 Nc5 Qc6

After 24...Bxc5 25 bxc5 White can put pressure down the b-file with Rb2.

25 a4!

Preventing ...Nb5. Now Black's knight on a7 has a bleak future.

25...b6 26 Nd3

But not 26 Nxa6? Qc4!, leaving White's knight rather marooned on a6.

26...Kg8 27 h4 Qd7 28 g5 Rc3 29 h5!

Finally White initiates proceedings on the kingside.

29...gxh5 30 Nf4 Rxe3

30...g6 31 Nxg6! is very strong, as 31...fxg6 32 Qxg6+ Kh8 33 Rh2 will deliver mate.

31 Nxh5 Qc6 32 Nf6+! Bxf6

32...gxf6 33 gxf6 is disastrous for Black, who cannot prevent 34 Rg2+ Kh8 35 Rh2+ Kg8 36 Qh7 mate.

33 gxf6 g6

Now White just needs to get his queen to h6...

34 Rc2!? Qd7? (Diagram 14)

34...Rc3 loses to 35 Qc1! Rxc2 36 Qh6, so 34...Qxa4 was Black's last chance.

35 Qc1! Black resigns

If the rook on e3 moves, White will play Qh6 and Qg7 mate.

Summary

1) The Rossolimo and Moscow Variations are good choices for those disinclined to learn the theory associated with Open Sicilians.

2) Note that those wishing to use these systems would also require a response to the move order 1 e4 c5 2 Nf3 e6.

3) These lines tend to lead to quieter and more closed positions than the ones associated with Open Sicilians. Positional nuance is likely to be more important that tactical prowess.

Chapter Eight

The c3 Sicilian

1 e4 c5 2 c3 (Diagram 1)

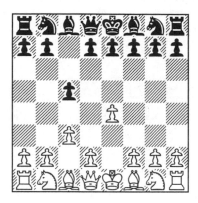

Diagram 1
The c3 Sicilian

From modest beginnings, the c3 Sicilian has in the last couple of decades catapulted itself to become the leading option for white players wishing to steer clear of Open Sicilians. It has many things going for it: it's logical, reliable and it doesn't require too much learning. Instead of having to worry about which of the many variations of the Open Sicilian he is likely to get, the c3 Sicilian practitioner forces his opponent into his territory as early as move two.

The c3 Sicilian is built on a positionally sound basis. White wishes to erect a pawn centre with d2-d4, supported by the pawn on c3. If Black captures after d2-d4 White, naturally, will recapture with the c-pawn thus keeping his centre intact. Of course, this is what would happen in an ideal world. In the real world Black also has moves and we shall be looking at the most important ones in this chapter.

If there is a weakness to White's second move, it's that it doesn't help White's development. Furthermore, c2-c3 also deprives White's b1-knight of its most natural square. Both of Black's main two options take advantage of this fact.

Black plays 2...d5

1 e4 c5 2 c3 d5 (Diagram 2)

Black strikes out in the centre with his d-pawn, attacking White's pawn on e4. White is forced to react immediately.

3 exd5

3 e5 is possible, but not to be recommended. After 3...Bf5! 4 d4 e6 Black has a very good version of the Advance Variation of the French Defence. Normally the light-squared bishop is locked behind the f7/e6/d5 pawn chain, but here it is actively placed on f5.

3...Qxd5

147

Normally it's not a good idea to bring the queen out into the centre of the board so early as you can easily lose time when it's chased around the board. Here, however, White cannot attack the queen in the usual way with Nc3 as this square is occupied by a pawn. Thus Black's queen can remain in the centre, for the time being at least.

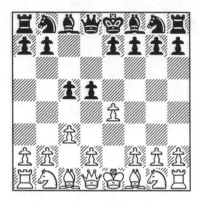

| **Diagram 2** | **Diagram 3** |
| Black plays 2...d5 | A common position from 2...d5 |

4 d4

The most logical continuation. White carries out his idea of d2-d4.

4...Nf6

Black develops a kingside piece. It's also possible to exert early pressure on the d4-pawn with 4...Nc6 5 Nf3 Bg4 but White has enough resources to protect it: 6 Be2 cxd4 7 cxd4 Bxf3? (7...e6 is okay for Black) 8 Bxf3 Qxd4?? would lose to 9 Bxc6+ bxc6 10 Qxd4.

5 Nf3 e6

Developing the bishop outside the pawn chain with 5...Bg4 is Black's main alternative (see Game 51).

6 Be3

White can also continue with 6 Be2 or 6 Bd3, but the text move is more forcing. By attacking the c5-pawn, White encourages Black to exchange on d4, which will then free up the c3-square for the b1-knight.

6...cxd4 7 cxd4 Nc6 8 Nc3

Finally the queen is attacked and must retreat.

8...Qd6

The most popular choice, although 8...Qd8 and 8...Qa5 have also been played. On d6 the queen is fairly active, but it's close enough to home not to be hassled too much by the white pieces.

9 a3

White wishes to develop his light-squared bishop on d3, where it bears down the long b1-h7 diagonal. In particular, this piece can be an important attacking weapon when Black has castled kingside. The reason for a quick a2-a3 is so that the bishop is safeguarded from being attacked with ...Nb4.

9...Be7 10 Bd3 0-0 11 0-0 (Diagram 3)

Strategies

This is what's known as an Isolated Queen's Pawn (IQP) position and similar positions can arise from many different openings. The main feature is White's isolated pawn on d4, which has both positive and negative features. On the plus side, it grants White extra space and it controls useful squares. White has good chances of building up an initiative and often goes for an attack on the kingside. On the other hand, the pawn itself is a weakness as it cannot be protected by any other white pawns. Thus it needs to be protected by pieces, which in turn lose some of their attacking power. As the game goes on and exchanges are made, this weakness becomes more and more pronounced. So White has an early initiative and attacking chances, but if Black can neutralise this he has good chances of success later on. There are many examples of quick white wins, but also a number of longer games where Black finally wins that isolated pawn and makes his extra pawn count!

Theoretical?

Not particularly. A good appreciation of IQP positions is more important.

Statistics

I found over 12,000 examples of 2...d5 in *Mega Database 2002*, with White scoring 52%. The solidity of the this line is reflected in the number of draws, which top score on 38%, ahead of white wins (33%) and black wins (29%). Garry Kasparov is an adherent of 2...d5, although he did lose one famous game against the computer *Deep Blue* with it.

Illustrative Games

Game 50
□ **Palkovi** ■ **Danner**
Budapest 1995

1 e4 c5 2 c3 d5 3 exd5 Qxd5 4 d4 e6 5 Nf3 Nf6 6 Be3 cxd4 7 cxd4 Nc6 8 Nc3 Qd6 9 a3 Be7 10 Bd3 b6 11 0-0 Bb7 12 Qe2

Preparing to play Rad1, which will add further support to the d-pawn. This is not a defensive procedure but more of an aggressive one: with the rook behind the pawn White can always be on the lookout to break with d4-d5.

12...0-0 13 Rad1 Rfd8

Likewise, Black controls the d5-square, thus making it harder for White to achieve a d4-d5 breakthrough.

14 Rfe1

When the bishop moves from its rather passive posting on e3, the queen and rook will bear down on the half-open e-file.

14...Rac8 15 Bg5

Unleashing the power down the e-file and attacking one of Black's main defenders.

15...Nd5? (Diagram 4)

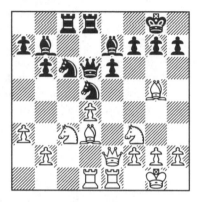

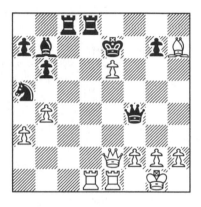

Diagram 4
Black's blockade is temporary

Diagram 5
White has a winning combination

Another example of moving the defensive knight being a mistake. Black blocks the d5-pawn, but tactics dictate that this is only a temporary defence. He should have either played 15...g6, blocking the b1-h7 diagonal, or 15...h6, putting the question to the bishop. For example: 15...h6 16 Bxf6!? Bxf6 17 d5 Nd4! (17...exd5 18 Nxd5 Qxd5? 19 Bh7+! Kxh7 20 Rxd5 Rxd5 21 Qe4+! wins for White) 18 Nxd4 Bxd4 19 dxe6 Qxe6 20 Qxe6 fxe6 with an equal endgame, Seger-Emms, German Bundesliga 2000.

16 Nxd5 Qxd5

This is forced, as 16...Bxg5 17 Nxg5 Qxd5 18 Qh5 is clearly disastrous for Black.

17 Be4!

The black queen must retreat, allowing White to break through with d4-d5. In this particular position this thrust is very effective.

17...Qd6

Or 17...Qd7 18 d5! exd5 19 Bxd5 (threatening Bxf7+, uncovering the rook on the queen) 19...Bxg5 20 Nxg5 Re8 21 Qxe8+! Rxe8 22 Rxe8+

Qxe8 23 Bxf7+ Qxf7 24 Nxf7 Kxf7 25 Rd7+ and White wins – Palkovi.

18 d5!

NOTE: The d4-d5 advance is often a powerful weapon in IQP positions.

18...Na5

18...exd5 19 Rxd5 wins material, for example 19...Qc7 20 Rxd8+ Qxd8 21 Bxc6 Bxc6 22 Bxe7.

19 b4! Bxg5

All the tactics work for White, for example: 19...Nc4 20 dxe6 Qxe6 21 Rxd8+ Rxd8 (or 21...Bxd8 22 Bxb7) 22 Bxe7 and White wins a piece.

20 Nxg5

Now White threatens the knight on a5 and the crucial h7-pawn. The game is already over as a contest.

20...Qf4 21 Bxh7+ Kf8 22 Nxe6+!

White has other ways to win, but this piece sacrifice is the most deadly.

22...fxe6 23 dxe6 Ke7 (Diagram 5)

Or 23...Rxd1 24 e7+ Ke8 25 Bg6+ Kd7 26 e8Q+ Rxe8 27 Qxe8+ Kc7 28 Rxd1 and White wins.

24 Rd7+! Rxd7 25 exd7+ Kxd7 26 Qe7+ Kc6 27 bxa5 Rc7 28 Be4+ Black resigns

White wins comfortably after 28...Kb5 29 Qb4+ Ka6 30 Bd3+.

Game 51
□ **Egin** ■ **Mukhametov**
Omsk 1996

---

1 e4 c5 2 c3 d5 3 exd5 Qxd5 4 d4 Nf6 5 Nf3 Bg4

This is a very reliable move. Black pins the knight on f3 and increases the pressure on d4.

6 Be2

Unpinning the knight is the most popular choice, but White has also tried 6 Nbd2, 6 Qa4+ and 6 dxc5.

6...e6 7 h3 Bh5 8 0-0 Nc6 9 Be3

Once again forcing Black to make a decision with his c5-pawn.

9...cxd4 10 cxd4

White takes on the isolated pawn. A more solid approach is 10 Nxd4 Bxe2 11 Qxe2 Be7 12 Rd1 0-0 with a level position.

10...Be7 11 Nc3 Qd6

Again Black takes up this useful square with the queen.

12 a3

White wants to play Qb3 without allowing Black the opportunity to offer the exchange of queens with ...Qb4.

12...0-0 13 Qb3 Rac8 14 Rfd1

14 Qxb7?! Rb8 15 Qa6 Rxb2 is not a good pawn swap for White; Black's rook on b2 is very active.

14...Nd5 (Diagram 6)

Black can also move his king's rook into the action with 14...Rfd8.

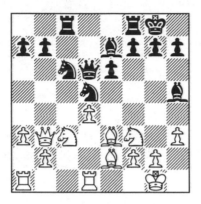

Diagram 6	Diagram 7
Black blockades the d4-pawn	White's knight is a spectator

15 Ne4

15 Nxd5 Qxd5 (or 15...exd5!?) 16 Qxd5 exd5 leaves us with a level ending.

15...Qb8 16 Rac1 Rfd8 17 Nc5?!

The beginning of a strange knight manoeuvre.

17...b6 18 Na6?

This knight is totally out of place on a6, where it stays for the rest of the game. White should have been content with just retreating back to e4.

NOTE: In general, the knight is much more effective in the centre than on the edge.

18...Qd6 19 Qa4 Bf6 20 Rc4 Nce7 21 Rdc1 Rxc4 22 Rxc4 Nxe3!

Creating a weakness on e3.

23 fxe3 Nf5

Black naturally plays on the kingside, where he has an extra piece. White could do with moving that knight from a6 to f1!

24 Rc3 Bxf3! 25 Bxf3 (Diagram 7) 25...Nxe3!

Black wins material with a fairly straightforward combination.

26 Rxe3 Bxd4 27 Qb3 Qf4 28 Kf2 Bxe3+ White resigns

After 29 Qxe3 Rd2+! Black wins the queen.

Black plays 2...Nf6

1 e4 c5 2 c3 Nf6 (Diagram 8)

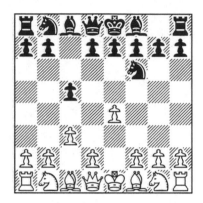

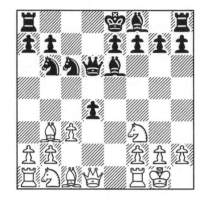

Diagram 8	Diagram 9
Black plays 2...Nf6	The main line with 2...Nf6

Another very logical move, attacking White's e4-pawn and again making use of the fact that White cannot play Nc3.

3 e5

This is virtually forced. The move 3 d3 would be totally out of character with White's second move.

3...Nd5

The best square for the knight. But not 3...Ne4?? 4 d3! and the knight is trapped in the middle of the board.

4 d4

White carries out his main idea. Instead he could continue to attack the knight with 4 c4 Nb4 5 a3 N4c6. However, it's not really clear what White has gained by doing this and now the e5-pawn lacks any real support.

4...cxd4 5 Nf3

White could also capture immediately with 5 cxd4, which would most likely transpose into the note to White's sixth move after 5...d6 6 Nf3 Nc6.

An independent try is 5 Qxd4 but this is not particularly popular. After Black defends his knight with 5...e6 he will gain time attacking the white queen with ...Nc6.

5...Nc6

Another important move here is 5...e6 (see Game 53). Of course, 5...dxc3?? loses a piece to 6 Qxd5.

6 Bc4

This gambit has been considered as the main variation for quite a few years now. The older line runs 6 cxd4 d6 7 Bc4 Nb6 (7...e6 is also possible and transposes to Game 53) 8 Bb5 dxe5 9 Nxe5 Bd7 with a reasonably quiet and level position. One continuation is 10 Bxc6 Bxc6 11 Nxc6 bxc6 12 0-0 g6 13 Re1 Bg7 14 Bg5 0-0!? 15 Bxe7 Qxd4 16 Qxd4 Bxd4 and the endgame is equal.

Exercise 8: Is 17 Bxf8 a good move?

6...Nb6

6...e6 7 cxd4 d6 again transposes to Game 53.

7 Bb3 d5

By far the most popular choice. Black strikes in the centre and opens lines for his pieces. It's certainly possible to grab the pawn with 7...dxc3 8 Nxc3 but hardly anyone seems prepared to play this position with Black. It's true that White has open lines and fast development (this looks like a favourable version of the Morra Gambit – see Chapter 9).

8 exd6

White can regain his pawn with 8 cxd4, but this allows Black comfortable development with 8...Bg4 followed by ...e7-e6.

8...Qxd6

Again the most common choice. The line 8...dxc3 9 Nxc3 exd6 gives Black an extra pawn, but White gets a strong initiative, for example: 10 Ng5 d5 11 0-0 Be7 12 Qh5 g6 13 Qh6 and Black is already under heavy pressure.

9 0-0

White continues in gambit style. Again White can regain his pawn, but after 9 cxd4 Be6 10 0-0 Bxb3 11 Qxb3 e6 12 Nc3 Be7 Black develops easily.

9...Be6! (Diagram 9)

Aiming to trade off White's attacking bishop.

9...dxc3 is very risky, as after 10 Nxc3 Qxd1 11 Rxd1 White keeps a strong initiative despite the exchange of queens, for example: 11...a6 (White was threatening Nb5) 12 Be3! Nd7 13 Nd5! and Black is in big trouble.

Strategies

White now has a major choice. He can exchange on e6 and recapture on d4, leading to a reasonably level position, or he can make it a real gambit by playing 10 Na3 (see Game 52). Positions after 10 Na3 are extremely sharp and no real conclusions have been drawn. Sometimes White even sacrifices a second pawn for a further developmental advantage, but it should be said that Black's structure remains pretty resilient to attack.

Theoretical?

In general the variations in the c3-Sicilian are non-theoretical, but this main line is an exception. The 2...Nf6 lines are in the main sharper than those with 2...d5 and black players need to read up before accepting too many pawns!

Statistics

I found over 10,000 games in *Mega Database 2002*, with Black scoring an impressive 51%. This figure is tempered by the fact that on average the black players were higher rated. This also seems to suggest that 2...Nf6 is used by the stronger player when he is going all out for a win. However, despite everything, the draw still top scores with 35%.

Illustrative Games

Game 52
□ **Benjamin** ■ **Ilincic**
Yerevan Olympiad 1996

1 e4 c5 2 c3 Nf6 3 e5 Nd5 4 d4 cxd4 5 Nf3 Nc6 6 Bc4 Nb6 7 Bb3 d5 8 exd6 Qxd6 9 0-0 Be6 10 Na3

White chooses to sacrifice. The alternative is 10 Bxe6 Qxe6 11 Nxd4 Nxd4 12 Qxd4 Rd8 with a fairly level position.

10...dxc3 11 Qe2

Offering a second pawn to keep the queens on the board.

11...Bxb3

Eliminating White's attacking bishop. 11...cxb2 12 Bxb2 may be playable, but White's initiative is looking more and more threatening.

12 Nb5

White attacks the black queen before recapturing on b3.

NOTE: An in-between move before an obvious one (like a recapture) is known as a Zwischenzug.

12...Qb8 13 axb3 e5 (Diagram 10)

Preparing to develop the bishop and castle kingside. Note that Black is not interested in grabbing another pawn on b2 as this would only bring White's c1-bishop to life.

14 bxc3

White has other interesting choices here, including 14 Bf4, 14 Re1, 14 Nfd4 and 14 Nbd4. Plenty for the black player to learn!

14...Be7 15 Bg5 f6 16 Be3 Nc8

16...0-0?! 17 Nxa7! Rxa7 18 Bxb6 regains the pawn and leaves White with an advantage.

17 Nh4 0-0

Black has survived the first wave of attack and has managed to castle. However, he must still be careful as the earlier ...f7-f6 has weakened his kingside.

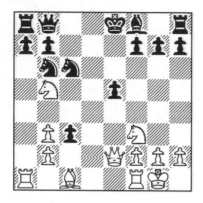

Diagram 10	Diagram 11
Black must complete development	Black has a small advantage

18 Qg4

Preparing to threaten mate with Nf5.

18...a6 19 Nf5 g6 20 Nxe7+ N6xe7!

The correct recapture. 20...N8xe7 allows White's knight into the d6-square after 21 Qe6+ Kg7 22 Nd6.

21 Qc4+ Kg7!

Again Black must be very careful. 21...Rf7 allows a very strong attack with 22 Rad1! axb5 23 Rd8+ Kg7 24 Bh6+! Kxh6 25 Qxf7 with a nasty threat of Rh8.

22 Nc7 Nd6 23 Qc5 Rc8 24 Nxa8

Or 24 Qxd6 Qxc7 and Black has defended successfully, although this ending is also fine for Black.

24...Rxc5 25 Bxc5 Ne4! 26 Bxe7 Qxa8 (Diagram 11)

Black has a queen and a pawn for two rooks – a reasonably fair trade.

27 Bb4 Kf7 28 Rfe1 f5 29 Re2 Qd8 30 f3 Qb6+ 31 Kf1 Nc5 32 Rd1

Ilincic gives the line 32 Rxe5! Nd3 33 Re2 Nxb4 34 cxb4 Qxb4 35 Re3! with a draw being the likely result. The rest of the game sees Black slowly converting his slight advantage.

32...Ke6 33 Bxc5 Qxc5 34 c4 Qa3 35 Rd3 h5 36 g3 g5 37 Rd5 Qa1+ 38 Kf2 f4! 39 gxf4 gxf4 40 Kg2 Qc3 41 h4 b5 42 Red2 bxc4 43 Rd8 Qb4 44 bxc4 Qe7 45 Kh3 a5 46 Rg8 a4 47 Rg6+ Kf7 48 Rh6 Qf8 49 Rc6 Qa3 50 Rc7+ Ke6 51 Kg2 Qe3 52 Rcd7 Qc5 53 Rh7 e4 54 Rh6+ Ke7 55 Rd5 exf3+ 56 Kh3 Qc8+ 57 Kh2 Qg4 58 Rh7+ Ke6 59 Rh6+ Kf7 60 Rh7+ Kg6 White resigns

Game 53
□ **Howell** ■ **Ward**
Norwich 1994

1 e4 c5 2 c3 Nf6 3 e5 Nd5 4 Nf3 e6 5 d4 cxd4 6 cxd4 d6 7 Bc4

It's also possible to play Bf1-d3, but White normally precedes this move with a2-a3 preventing an annoying knight coming to b4.

7...Nc6 8 0-0 Be7 9 Qe2 0-0 10 Nc3!?

A double-edged move. White accepts structural weaknesses in return for obvious attacking chances on the kingside. Another way to play is with 10 Qe4 preparing to set up mating threats with Bd3.

10...Nxc3 11 bxc3 dxe5 12 dxe5 (Diagram 12)

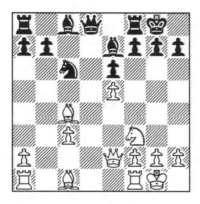

Diagram 12	Diagram 13
White accepts weaknesses	White has a very strong move

Now the c3-pawn is isolated and also the e5-pawn can sometimes become vulnerable. In return, all of White's pieces are active and he has very good chances to amount an attack against the black king.

12...Qc7 13 Qe4

With the idea of Bd3 and possibly Ng5 or Bg5.

13...b6

Preparing to fianchetto the bishop.

14 Bg5! Bxg5?!

Perhaps Black could defend better here with 14...Bb7 15 Bd3 g6 16 Qh4 Rfe8.

15 Nxg5 g6

The only decent way to prevent mate, but now Black has some dark-squared weaknesses around his king.

16 Rae1!

Protecting the vulnerable e5-pawn.

16...h6? (Diagram 13)

This allows a neat combination. The line 16...Nxe5 17 Qxe5 Qxc4 wins a pawn, but after 18 Ne4! White has a nasty threat of Nf6+. Probably Black's best move was 16...Bb7!.

17 Bxe6! Kg7

Or:

1) 17...fxe6 18 Nxe6! Bxe6 19 Qxg6+ Kh8 20 Qxh6+ Qh7 21 Qxe6 leaves White with four pawns for the knight and Black's king has no cover whatsoever.

2) 17...hxg5 18 Qxg6+ Kh8 19 Qh6+ Kg8 20 Qxg5+ Kh8 21 Qf6+ Kg8 22 Re4 Bxe6 23 Rh4 and White mates on h8.

18 Bxf7! Rxf7 19 Nxf7 Kxf7 20 e6+

Black has two pieces for a rook and two pawns, which is normally a reasonable trade. Here, however, his pieces are too far away to protect the king and White's attack steams on.

20...Kg7 21 f4!

Preparing f4-f5.

21...Ba6 22 Rf2 Qd6 23 f5 Bd3 24 f6+! Kh7 25 Qe3

Now White has two monstrous passed pawns on the sixth rank. The result is not in doubt.

NOTE: Two connected and passed pawns on the sixth rank are usually decisive.

25...Bc4 26 Rd2 Qc5 27 Qxc5 bxc5 28 Rd7+ Kg8 29 Rc7 Nd8 30 Rxa7!

A nice trick. 30...Rxa7 31 e7 and the e-pawn promotes.

30...Rb8 31 e7 Ne6 32 e8Q+! Black resigns

32...Rxe8 33 f7+ wins easily.

Summary

1) The c3 Sicilian is an excellent alternative for those wishing to avoid the complexities of the Open Sicilian.

2) Pawn structures are very different from the normal Open Sicilian. Often White ends up with an isolated queen's pawn.

3) 2...d5 is reliable, especially in conjunction with 5...Bg4 (see Game 51).

4) 2...Nf6 generally leads to sharper lines, especially when White plays the gambit line.

Chapter Nine

Other Systems

- The Closed Sicilian
- The Grand Prix Attack
- The Morra Gambit

The Closed Sicilian

1 e4 c5 2 Nc3 Nc6 3 g3 (Diagram 1)

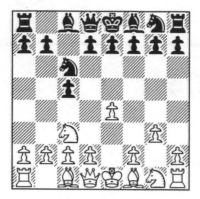

Diagram 1	Diagram 2
The Closed Sicilian	A typical Closed Sicilian

The Closed Sicilian leads to positions which are just that ...closed! Pawn exchanges in the opening and early middlegame are rare and both sides slowly manoeuvre behind their pawn structures.

White's second move is to prevent Black from playing an early ...d7-d5 (2 g3 can be met by 2...d5!?). It should be said that although 2...Nc6 is by far Black's most popular move, 2...d6 and 2...e6 are also playable. An example of the latter is 2...e6 3 g3 d5 4 exd5 exd5 5 Bg2 Nf6 6 d3 d4 7 Ne4 Nxe4 8 dxe4 with a roughly level position.

3...g6

Fianchettoing the f8-bishop is Black's most common approach.

4 Bg2 Bg7 5 d3 d6 6 Be3

In the last few years this move has superseded 6 f4 (see Game 55) as the main line. White can play in 'Yugoslav Attack' style with Qd2 and, when the g8-knight develops, White can swap bishops with Bh6.

6...Rb8

Black prepares ...b7-b5, beginning queenside counterplay. Another way forward is development with 6...e6 7 Qd2 Nge7, when White should offer the exchange of bishops. One possible continuation is 8 Bh6 0-0 9 Bxg7 Kxg7 10 h4!?, preparing a quick attack with h4-h5.

7 Qd2 b5

Notice that Black delays the development of the g8-knight so that White doesn't have the easy plan of Be3-h6.

8 Nge2 Nd4

Black plants his knight into a very useful outpost and prevents White from playing d3-d4. At the moment White isn't in a good position to exchange it. 9 Bxd4 cxd4 10 Nd1 means that White has to give up his Bh6 ideas, while 9 Nxd4?? cxd4 simply loses a piece to the pawn fork.

NOTE: ...Nc6-d4 is a typical manoeuvre for Black in the Closed Sicilian.

9 0-0 b4

Gaining extra space on the queenside and forcing the c3-knight to retreat. Notice the influence the g7-bishop has along the long diagonal. This is why White would ideally like to trade it for his e3-bishop.

10 Nd1 (Diagram 2)

Strategies

A highly tense position has arisen. White has two immediate plans: one is to get rid of that knight on d4; the second is to try to force the exchange of dark-squared bishops. The first can be carried out by a c2-c3 advance, inducing Black to exchange on e2. However, more often White actually moves the e2 knight away before proceeding with c2-c3, thus keeping pieces on the board and forcing the d4-knight back. At some point Black must complete his development, but he may choose to keep his knight on g8 for the time being, preventing White from playing Be3-h6. Black may expand further on the queenside with moves such as ...a7-a5 and ...Ba6.

Theoretical?

The 6 Be3 lines are less theoretical than those with 6 f4, if only because the lines are more modern and firm conclusions have yet to be drawn. A good understanding of these closed positions is much more important than learning some moves in parrot fashion.

Statistics

The Closed Sicilian is a big favourite of the ex-World Champion Boris Spassky, while more recently it has been taken up by Michael Adams and Nigel Short.

Taking the early position after 3...g6 in the main line, I found nearly 16,000 examples in *Mega Database 2002*, with White scoring a rather miserable 47%, although black players were higher rated on average.

Illustrative Games

Game 54
☐ **Short** ■ **Hossain**
Dhaka 1999

1 e4 c5 2 Nc3 Nc6 3 g3 g6 4 Bg2 Bg7 5 d3 d6 6 Be3 Rb8 7 Qd2 b5 8 Nge2 Nd4 9 0-0 b4 10 Nd1 e6

Black prepares to complete kingside development with ...Nge7 and ...0-0. Other possibilities include expansion on the queenside with 10...a5 and an immediate exchange of the knight on e2.

11 Nc1

Preparing to kick the d4-knight away without allowing exchanges. White's knights look a little strange lined up on the back rank, but they eventually re-enter the game.

11...Ne7 12 c3 bxc3 13 bxc3 Ndc6

The first objective has been achieved. Now White exchanges the dark-squared bishops.

14 Bh6! (Diagram 3)

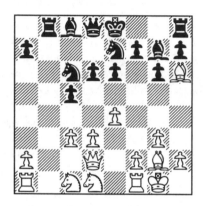

Diagram 3
White offers an exchange of bishops

Diagram 4
White crashes through

14...0-0 15 Bxg7 Kxg7 16 Ne3 e5 17 Ne2

White has two possible pawn breaks: d3-d4 and f2-f4. Black's next move takes measures against the first of these, so Short opts for f2-f4.

17...Ba6 18 f4! f6 19 Rac1 Qa5

Of course, Black strives for counterplay on the queenside.

20 Rc2 Rb7 21 Bh3!

The e6-square will be a very useful outpost for this bishop.

21...Rfb8 22 Be6 Rb1 23 Nc1!

An important move. White needs to keep pieces on the board in order for his kingside attack to work. An exchange of rooks would have favoured Black.

23...Qb6 24 Qf2 Rf8 25 h4 Qd8 26 f5

White's attack on the kingside is proving to be more effective than Black's on the other wing. Black now tries a speculative sacrifice to gain counterplay but the position only opens up in White's favour.

26...Rxc1? 27 Rfxc1 Bxd3 28 Rd2 Bxe4 29 Rcd1

Black has a knight and two pawns for a rook, which is often a fair trade. Here, however, Black is still passive and he has problems defending down the d-file.

29...Nc8 30 Nc4 Bxf5 31 Bxf5 gxf5 32 Nxd6 (Diagram 4)

The d6-pawn goes and Black's position collapses.

32...Nxd6 33 Rxd6 Qc8 34 Rd7+ Black resigns

White will follow up with Qxf5.

Game 55
□ **Spassky** ■ **Gufeld**
Wellington 1988

---

1 e4 c5 2 Nc3 Nc6 3 g3 g6 4 Bg2 Bg7 5 d3 d6 6 f4

The older move. White erects a pawn front on the kingside and hopes for a slow-burning attack in that direction.

6...e6

Once again Black opts to develop his knight on e7.

7 Nf3 Nge7 8 0-0 0-0 9 Be3 Nd4

Again we see this ...Nd4 move, preventing White from carrying out a d3-d4 advance.

10 e5

This move breathed new life into the Closed Sicilian in the 1980s, with players such as Spassky scoring impressive wins with it. It's certainly easy for Black to go wrong, even if he plays natural-looking moves.

NOTE: 10 e5 is a dangerous sacrificial idea.

10...Nef5 11 Bf2 Nxf3+ 12 Qxf3 Nd4 13 Qd1 dxe5 14 fxe5 Bxe5 15 Ne4! (Diagram 5)

This is the point. The knight attacks the c5-pawn and White will follow up with c2-c3, assuring that he will recover the pawn.

15...f5

Black cannot protect his pawn: 15...b6 loses material after 16 c3 Nf5 17 Nf6+ Bxf6 18 Bxa8.

16 Nxc5

Now if Black does nothing White will quickly follow up with c2-c3 and d3-d4, establishing a formidable central structure.

16...Qd6 17 b4! Rb8?

After this move White develops a clear advantage. Much stronger is 16...Nc6! 17 Rb1 Bd4! (exchanging bishops) 18 Qd2 Bxf2+ 19 Qxf2 Rb8 20 a3 b6 and Black had reached a playable position in Spassky-Hjartarson, European Club Cup 1991.

18 c3 Nb5 19 d4 Bf6 20 Qb3 b6 21 Nd3 Bb7?!

This exchange doesn't help Black as his e6-pawn now becomes vulnerable.

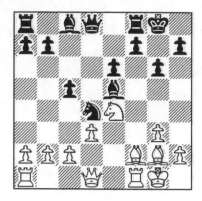

Diagram 5
White attacks c5

Diagram 6
White has a powerful sacrifice

22 Bxb7 Rxb7 23 a4 Nc7 24 Rfe1 Nd5?! 25 c4 Ne7 26 Nf4 Nc6 27 Rxe6 Qxb4 28 Qd3 Ne7 29 Be1 Qb2 30 Bc3 Qb3 (Diagram 6) 31 Rxf6!

This temporary sacrifice is decisive. Black will be murdered on the weak dark squares around his king.

31...Rxf6 32 d5 Kf7

Or 32...Rd6 33 Qd4 and the black king cannot escape, for example: 33...Kf7 34 Ne6 Ke8 35 Qh8+ Kd7 36 Qd8 mate.

33 Ne6 Rxe6

Or 33...Rd7 34 Nd4! and the black queen is trapped.

34 dxe6+ Kxe6 35 Re1+ Kf7 36 Qd4 Qxa4 37 Qg7+ Ke8 38 Bf6 Kd8 39 Qf8+ Qe8 40 Rd1+ Rd7 41 Bxe7+ Kc7 42 Qxe8 Black resigns

The Grand Prix Attack

1 e4 c5 2 Nc3 Nc6 3 f4 (Diagram 7)

White prepares to play in a similar manner to the f4 lines of the Closed Sicilian, the major difference being that White will be looking to develop his f1-bishop more actively on c4 or b5. The Grand Prix is more popular (and perhaps more powerful) when Black has already committed himself with 2...d6 (see Game 57).

White can also play an immediate 2 f4, but then Black has the extra option of 2...d5.

3...g6

Black has various ways to play but the kingside fianchetto is the most common.

4 Nf3 Bg7 5 Bb5

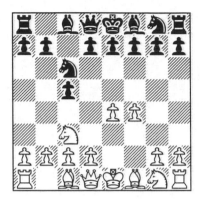

Diagram 7

The Grand Prix Attack

Diagram 8

Black plays ...Nd4

Putting pressure on the c6-knight and preparing to castle. White may intend to capture on c6 to give Black doubled c-pawns.

The main alternative is 5 Bc4, bearing down on the f7-square. However, Black can blunt this attack with 5...e6 preparing to kick the bishop away with ...d7-d5 (5...d6 would transpose to Game 57, but it makes more sense to go for ...d7-d5). The main line is very complex: 6 f5!? Nge7 (Black ignores the pawn offer as he doesn't want to ruin his structure) 7 fxe6 fxe6 (7...dxe6 is safe and solid if Black is looking for an easy life) 8 d3 d5 9 Bb3 b5 10 exd5 exd5 11 0-0 (11 Nxb5 Qa5+ 12 Nc3 c4! is good for Black) 11...c4 12 dxc4 dxc4 13 Qxd8+ Nxd8 14 Nxb5 cxb3 15 Nc7+ Kd7 16 Nxa8 bxc2 with massive complications.

5...Nd4! (Diagram 8)

The main response. Black hops his knight into the central outpost and prevents an exchange on c6.

Strategies

White has several possibilities in this position. He can move his bishop, support it with a2-a4, exchange on d4 or simply castle. Black needs to complete development on the kingside and would like to play ...d7-d6 and ...Nf6, but this can only be done after the bishop is removed from b5.

Theoretical?

The Grand Prix Attack is quite popular at club level but less so at international level, so there's not a vast amount of theory which has been established and there is certainly scope for introducing new ideas.

Statistics

In over 7,000 games in *Mega Database 2002*, White scored poorly with 49%, but on this occasion black players were significantly higher rated on average.

Illustrative Games

Game 56
□ **Hodgson** ■ **Petursson**
Reykjavik 1989

1 e4 c5 2 Nc3 Nc6 3 f4 g6 4 Nf3 Bg7 5 Bb5 Nd4 6 Nxd4

White goes for an immediate exchange on d4. More popular recently has been 6 0-0, for example: 6...a6 7 Bd3 d6 8 Nxd4 cxd4 9 Ne2 Nf6 10 Kh1 Nd7 11 b4 0-0 12 Bb2 Qb6 13 Rb1 Nb8 14 c3 Nc6 15 h3 Be6 16 a4 Rac8 with an equal position in Adams-Anand, Groningen (6th matchgame) 1997. In fact the main game is similar, but Black does not expend a tempo with ...a7-a6, which is probably to his advantage.

6...cxd4 7 Ne2 Nf6

Attacking the e4-pawn.

8 Bd3

Exercise 9: What does Black play against 8 d3 here?

8...d6 9 0-0

After 9 Nxd4 Black regains his pawn with 9...Nxe4!, uncovering an attack on the d4-knight.

9...0-0 10 c3 dxc3 11 bxc3 (Diagram 9)

Now White plans Bc2 and d2-d4, with three pawns abreast in the centre.

11...b6!

This move, preparing to attack the e4-pawn with ...Bb7, prevents White from carrying out his intended idea.

12 Bc2 Bb7 13 d3 Qc7 14 Kh1 Rac8 15 f5?

White naturally goes for a kingside attack, but this turns out to be premature as Black has a big punch in the centre. More circumspect was 15 Qe1.

15...d5!

White's position was not ready for this central blow.

NOTE: A central strike is generally a good answer to a flank attack.

16 Bf4 Qc6! 17 Ba4 b5 18 Nd4 Qc5! 19 e5

19 Nxb5 dxe4 sees the end of White's impressive centre, so Hodgson decides to speculate.

19...bxa4 20 exf6 Bxf6 21 fxg6 hxg6 22 Qg4? Qxc3!

Calm defence. White's attack looks threatening but comes to nothing.

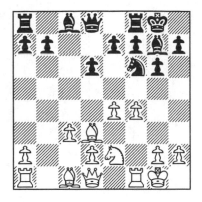

Diagram 9	**Diagram 10**
White plans Bc2 and d2-d4	Black takes over the operation

23 Nf5 Qxd3 24 Nh6+ Kg7 25 Rad1

Or 25 Nf5+ Kh7! and there is no good way to continue.

25...Qa3! 26 Nf5+ Kg8 27 h4 Rc4! (Diagram 10)

Slowly, but surely, Black starts to make his extra material count.

28 h5 g5 29 Rf3 Qb4 30 Rdf1 Bc8! 31 Nh6+ Kh7 32 Qg3 Rxf4 33 Rxf4 gxf4 White resigns

---

Game 57
□ **Short** ■ **Gelfand**
Brussels (3rd matchgame) 1991

---

1 e4 c5 2 Nc3 d6 3 f4 Nc6 4 Nf3 g6 5 Bc4

Bc4 is more logical when Black has already committed his d-pawn to d6 as he would have to expend another tempo to play ...d6-d5.

5...Bg7 6 0-0 e6 7 d3 Nge7 8 Qe1

From here the queen can go to h4, where it helps in an eventual king-side attack.

8...Nd4

By hitting the newly undefended c2-pawn, Black forces an exchange of knights. Also possible is 8...0-0.

9 Nxd4 cxd4 10 Ne2 0-0 11 Bb3 Nc6

Aiming to exchange the bishop off with ...Na5 and ...Nxb3. Short's next move prevents this.

12 Bd2 d5 13 e5 (Diagram 11)

White's bishop on b3 is now blocked out of the game but on the other hand White has a powerful pawn wedge on e5 and Black has to be careful not to weaken the dark squares around his own king.

13...f6 14 exf6 Bxf6 15 Kh1!

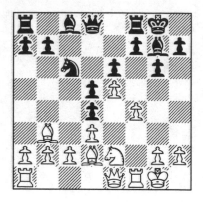

Diagram 11	Diagram 12
White has a pawn wedge on e5	White can deliver a decisive blow

An excellent move. White eyes the e5-outpost and plans the imaginative manoeuvre Ng1-f3.

15...a5 16 a4

Black was threatening to win a piece with ...a5-a4.

16...Qd6 17 Ng1 Bd7 18 Nf3 Nb4

Gelfand opts for queenside play, but it might have been wiser playing in the centre with 18...Rae8, as Short suggests. After 18...Nb4 Short cleverly keeps Gelfand's counterplay at bay while building up his forces on the kingside.

19 Qf2! Qc5 20 Bc3!

Using the pin against the black queen. The b4-knight must retreat.

20...Nc6 21 Rae1 b6 22 Bd2 Nb4?!

Again Black should probably go for 22...Rae8!.

23 Qg3 b5 24 f5!

This break leads to a very strong attack on the black king.

24...exf5

Or 24...bxa4 25 fxg6! axb3 26 gxh7+ Kxh7 (26...Kh8 27 Ne5 Bxe5 28 Qxe5+ Kxh7 29 Qh5+ Kg8 30 Qg6+ Kh8 31 Bf4 Nc6 32 Rf3 and Rh3 mate) 27 Ng5+ Bxg5 28 Qxg5 and Black is lost, for example: 28...bxc2 29 Qh4+ Kg8 30 Bh6 or 28...Rxf1+ 29 Rxf1 Rf8 30 Qh6+ Kg8 31 Qg6+ Kh8 32 Rf6 Qe7 33 Qh5+ Kg8 34 Rg6+ Kf7 35 Rg5+ Kf6 36 Qg6 mate.

25 Ne5 Be8?

Black's best chance is with 25...Ra7! 26 Nxd7 Rxd7 27 Rxf5 and White 'only' has a big advantage.

26 axb5 Qxb5 27 Rxf5 Kh8 (Diagram 12) 28 Rxf6!

Eliminating a dark-squared defender.

28...Rxf6 29 Ng4 Rf5 30 Nh6 Rh5 31 Qf4 Black resigns

Black cannot deal with the mate threats of Qf6 and Qf8. A very fine game by Short.

The Morra Gambit

1 e4 c5 2 d4 cxd4 3 c3 (Diagram 13)

Diagram 13
The Morra Gambit

Diagram 14
A typical Morra position

In contrast with 1 e4 e5 openings, White has very few gambit tries against the Sicilian. The Morra is one of White's more respected gambits, but is still seen relatively rarely at international level, the feeling being that Black has a few ways of finding a satisfactory game. However, as we shall see, the second player has to be quite careful in the opening stages.

The idea of the Morra is to offer a pawn for smooth development of the pieces. White usually obtains a useful development advantage and active posts for his pieces, but, as is normal in the Sicilian, Black's structure makes it difficult for White to initiate a successful attack.

3...dxc3

Black can also refuse the gambit pawn by playing 3...d3 or by transposing back into the c3 Sicilian with 3...Nf6 4 e5 Nd5.

4 Nxc3 Nc6 5 Nf3 d6

The move 5...e6 is another perfectly playable idea. A line that has caught more than one person out is the following: 6 Bc4 Qc7 7 0-0 Nf6 8 Qe2 Ng4! 9 h3?? Nd4! and White loses his queen as 10 Nxd4 Qh2 is mate. This is known as the Siberian Trap.

6 Bc4 e6

Sensibly blocking the bishop's path down to f7. For 6...Nf6?!, see Game 59.

7 0-0 Nf6 8 Qe2

Preparing Rd1 to pressurise the slightly weak d6-pawn.

8...Be7 9 Rd1 e5!

Otherwise White may exploit the pin on the d-file to play e4-e5 himself.

10 h3

A good prophylactic move, preventing Black from finding an active post for his c8-bishop with ...Bg4.

10...0-0 (Diagram 14)

Strategies

White will complete his development with moves such as Be3 (or Bg5) and Rac1. Black may try to neutralise the pressure on the a2-g8 diagonal with ...Be6 and prevent White's pieces coming to b5 with ...a7-a6. Black's extra pawn on d6 is vulnerable, but still performs defensive duties. Overall, Black's position is solid, but it will be difficult for him to exploit his extra pawn. White has just enough play for the pawn.

Theoretical?

Once Black has reached Diagram 14, he has avoided most of the traps, but Game 59 is a good illustration of how careful Black has to be in this opening.

Statistics

I found over 6,000 games in *Mega Database 2002*, with White scoring 48% but black players being significantly higher-rated. A high percentage of games (75%) were decisive.

Illustrative Games

Game 58
□ **Hardarson** ■ **Hjartarson**
Gardabaer 1991

1 e4 c5 2 d4 cxd4 3 c3 dxc3 4 Nxc3 Nc6 5 Nf3 d6 6 Bc4 e6 7 0-0 Nf6 8 Qe2 Be7 9 Rd1 e5 10 h3 0-0 11 Be3 a6

The immediate 11...Be6 is also possible: 12 Bxe6 fxe6 13 Rac1 Rc8 14 b4! a6 15 b5 axb5 16 Qxb5 Qd7 17 Na4 Nd4 18 Nxd4 exd4 19 Qxd7 Nxd7 20 Bxd4 resulted in an equal ending in Pokojowczyk-Gligoric, Yugoslavia 1971.

12 a4?!

The insertion of ...a7-a6 and a2-a4 seems to help Black as his move, preventing pieces coming to b5, is more useful. Perhaps White should simply continue development with 12 Rac1.

12...Be6

Now Black can play this move in more favourable circumstances.

13 Bxe6 fxe6 14 Qc4 Qd7 15 Ng5 Nd8 (Diagram 15)

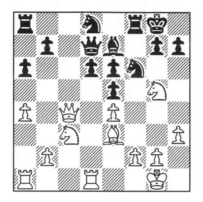
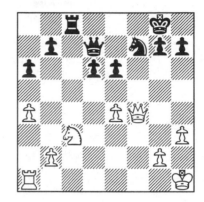

| **Diagram 15** | **Diagram 16** |
| Black sets up a solid defence | Black has an extra pawn |

16 f4?

This aggression backfires as Black is very well placed to meet it. 16 Bb6, intending to capture on d8, looks stronger although Black can keep his extra pawn after the continuation 16...Rc8 17 Qb3 h6 18 Bxd8 hxg5!.

16...exf4 17 Bxf4 Ng4

This discovered attack on the f4-bishop suddenly puts White right on the back foot.

18 Rf1

Black has a powerful answer to this, but White was already in trouble. 18 Bd2 is met by 18...b5! 19 axb5 Qa7+ 20 Kh1 Nf2+ and suddenly it's Black on the attack.

NOTE: Counterplay can be very swift in the Sicilian.

18...Rxf4 19 Rxf4 Ne3! 20 Qe2 Bxg5 21 Qxe3 Nf7

There is no rush to capture on f4 as the rook is pinned.

22 Kh1 Bxf4 23 Qxf4 Rc8 (Diagram 16)

Now Black is simply a clear pawn up for which White has no compensation.

24 Rd1 h6 25 Qe3 Qc6 26 Qd4 Qc5 27 Ne2 Qxd4 28 Nxd4

Or 28 Rxd4 Rc2, attacking the knight and b-pawn.

28...Ng5 29 b3 Nxe4 30 Re1 d5 White resigns

Black wins more material after 31 Nxe6 Re8 32 Nf4 Ng3+!.

Game 59
□ **Kristiansson** ■ **Roberts**
Harrachov 1967

1 e4 c5 2 d4 cxd4 3 c3 dxc3 4 Nxc3 Nc6 5 Nf3 d6 6 Bc4 Nf6?!

A natural-looking move, but it plays right into the hands of a Morra Gambit expert!

7 e5!

This move plunges Black into very early difficulties.

7...dxe5

7...Nxe5?? loses immediately to the trick 8 Nxe5 dxe5 9 Bxf7+! Kxf7 10 Qxd8.

8 Qxd8+ Nxd8

8...Kxd8 9 Ng5 is a big problem for Black, so he is forced to recapture with the knight.

9 Nb5! (Diagram 17)

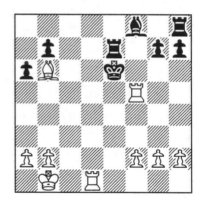

Diagram 17	**Diagram 18**
Black has a crisis	White can simplify

Suddenly the threat of Nc7+ forces Black into an early crisis. White's attack persists despite the exchange of queens.

9...Rb8 10 Nxe5 e6 11 Nc7+

11 Nxa7 is enough for an advantage, but White is looking for blood.

11...Ke7 12 Be3 Nc6 13 0-0-0!

Threatening mate in one with Bc5.

13...Nd7?

After this move White can win a couple of pawns and reach a decisive position. My computer program, *Fritz*, cannot come up with anything totally decisive against 13...Ne4, so I guess this is what Black should try.

NOTE: Tactically speaking, the computer is never wrong!

14 Nxf7! Kxf7 15 Bxe6+ Kg6 16 Bxd7 Bxd7 17 Rxd7

The smoke has cleared and White is a clear pawn ahead. Add this to White's more active pieces and Black's more 'active' king and we have a decisive plus for White.

17...Ne5 18 Rd5 Rc8 19 Rxe5 Rxc7+ 20 Kb1 a6 21 Rd1 Kf7 22 Bb6 Re7 23 Rf5+ Ke6 (Diagram 18) 24 Rxf8!

Simplifying to a winning king and pawn ending.

24...Rxf8 25 Re1+ Kd7 26 Rxe7+ Kxe7 27 Bc5+ Ke8 28 Bxf8 Kxf8 29 Kc2 Black resigns

Normally the advantage of one pawn is decisive in a king and pawn ending and this one is no different. One possible line is 29 Kc2 Ke7 30 Kd3 Ke6 31 Ke4 g6 32 f4 h5 33 g3 Kf6 34 h3 Ke6 35 g4 hxg4 36 hxg4 Kf6 37 f5 gxf5+ 38 gxf5 Kf7 39 Ke5 Ke7 40 f6+ Kf7 41 b4 Kf8 42 Kd6 Kf7 43 Kc7 Kxf6 44 Kxb7 Ke6 45 Kxa6 and the b-pawn promotes.

Summary

1) The Closed Sicilian is especially suitable for those players who prefer closed positions and dislike reaching critical positions until later on in the game.

2) The Grand Prix Attack is a tricky system and White can often build up serious kingside attacks.

3) The Morra Gambit is especially trappy but Black should be fine if he gets through the first few moves unscathed.

Solution to Exercises

Exercise 1: 14 Bh6 allows the tactic 14...Rxd4!, deflecting the white queen. After 15 Qxd4 Bxh6+ Black has won two minor pieces for a rook.

Exercise 2: The reply 12...Bb7!, skewering the queen to the rook, is a very effective reply for Black.

Exercise 3: Black plays 33...axb1N mate!.

Exercise 4: 26...Bf5 27 Qe2 f3 and the white queen can no longer defend c2 and c4 at the same time; White loses a piece.

Exercise 5: 23...Nxb2! crashes through White's defences as 24 Kxb2 Qxc3+ 25 Kb1 Qb2 is mate.

Exercise 6: 11...Nxc5? loses material after 12 Nxc6 Qxc6 (or 12...Nxa4 13 Nxe7) 13 Nxc5 Bxc5 14 Rc1 b6 15 b4 and the pinned bishop is lost.

Exercise 7: Black can trap the queen with 24...Rh8!. Did White miss this idea when giving up the pawn?

Exercise 8: The answer is no. Black can play 17...Bxb2!, regaining the rook with an extra pawn to boot. Instead White should play 17 Nc3 or 17 Nd2.

Exercise 9: 8...Qa5+! wins the bishop on b5.

Index of Complete Games